D0269891

DANNY DYER
East End Boy

DANNY DYER
East End Boy

Joe Allan

MICHAEL O'MARA BOOKS LIMITED

First published in Great Britain in 2014 by
Michael O'Mara Books Limited
9 Lion Yard
Tremadoc Road
London SW4 7NQ

Copyright © Michael O'Mara Books Limited 2014

All rights reserved. You may not copy, store, distribute, transmit, reproduce or otherwise make available this publication (or any part of it) in any form, or by any means (electronic, digital, optical, mechanical, photocopying, recording or otherwise), without the prior written permission of the publisher. Any person who does any unauthorized act in relation to this publication may be liable to criminal prosecution and civil claims for damages.

A CIP catalogue record for this book is available from the British Library. Papers used by Michael O'Mara Books Limited are natural, recyclable products made from wood grown in sustainable forests. The manufacturing processes conform to the environmental regulations of the country of origin.

ISBN: 978-1-78243-295-1 in hardback print format
ISBN: 978-1-78243-380-4 in trade paperback print format
ISBN: 978-1-78243-297-5 in e-book format

1 2 3 4 5 6 7 8 9 10

Designed and typeset by Design 23
Printed and bound by CPI Group (UK) Ltd, Croydon, CR0 4YY

www.mombooks.com

Contents

INTRODUCTION **EAST END BOY**   7

CHAPTER ONE **THE ARTFUL DODGER**   13

CHAPTER TWO **INTERCHANGE**   24

CHAPTER THREE **BABY LOVE**   32

CHAPTER FOUR **HIGHER THAN THE SUN**   39

CHAPTER FIVE **STAGE ONE**   56

CHAPTER SIX **ALL YOU NEED IS LOVE**   64

CHAPTER SEVEN **STAGE TWO**   77

CHAPTER EIGHT **FALLING IN LOVE AGAIN**   85

CHAPTER NINE **JUST FOR THE MONEY**   115

CHAPTER TEN **HEADING EAST**   151

CHAPTER ELEVEN **GET CARTER**   164

CHAPTER TWELVE **A FATHER AND SON STORY**   176

CHAPTER THIRTEEN **SOAPY BUBBLE**   189

CHAPTER FOURTEEN **THE FUTURE**   201

SOURCES   211
PICTURE ACKNOWLEDGEMENTS   214
INDEX   215

EAST END BOY

In 2007, Danny Dyer was preparing for the release of his latest film, *Straightheads*, a controversial revenge thriller in which he starred alongside former *X-Files* star, Gillian Anderson. At a relatively young age – he was just about to turn thirty – Danny was already considered an industry veteran, and *Straightheads* was just shy of being his twentieth film project. What he couldn't have known at the time was that, despite a career that would see him star in at least another twenty movies by the age of thirty-six, it would be, to date, one of his last films to enjoy a wide release in the UK's mainstream cinema chains, his future output relegated to preview screenings, limited cinema runs, video-on-demand and straight-to-DVD titles.

When interviewed for an article set to run on the LoveFilm website to coincide with the launch of the film, he was asked what his long-term ambitions were for his acting career. He insisted that he was always keen to stretch himself as an actor and keep his career moving forward. As he was on the verge of accepting his first job to shoot in America, he stated, 'Being on a soap for sixteen years would be my worst nightmare, like Ian Beale or Ken Barlow, who've been in the same role all those years.' He reasoned, 'I do understand that they have a nice house and a family – they've got their security. I ideally want to try something new, but, having said that, I'll probably end up working in *EastEnders* now, won't I . . . Give it ten years!'

Well, it wasn't quite ten years, but when it was announced in October 2013 that Danny Dyer would indeed be joining the cast of the BBC's flagship soap, *EastEnders*, many were outspokenly sceptical about his suitability, while others wondered if this would be the final nail in the struggling soap's coffin. Most speculated Danny would appear as a version of the clichéd East End gangster he had played in many of his films, just another two-dimensional villainous hard man – the kind of character that had become Danny's stock-in-trade over the previous decade. As if to address this assumption head-on, in his first interview with the BBC News website after his *EastEnders* sign-up was announced, Danny said of his new character, Mick Carter, 'There's definitely something there – you really don't want to cross him.' So far, so Mitchell brother, and certainly familiar territory for both *EastEnders* and Danny, but he went on to explain that, while there might be more to Mick than initially meets the eye – something darker and more dangerous – he was first and foremost a devoted husband and family man.

Mick was a father of three grown-up kids, 'a normal guy who loves his family', and 'a grafter'; even someone 'quite in touch with his feminine side'. On the surface at least, this appeared to be a refreshing change of pace for someone who had seen his reputation torn to shreds by the media, and one which, potentially, could be the role of a lifetime for someone who was the first to admit his career had been marred by some hasty decisions and bad choices, both professionally and personally.

Since making his television debut in 1993 as teenage rent boy Martin Fletcher alongside Helen Mirren in *Prime Suspect 3*, Danny Dyer has acted in over forty feature films, appeared in numerous television dramas and comedies, hosted documentary series and taken to the London stage in a handful of well-received stage roles. Over the years he has made a name for himself as the poster boy for Britain's low-budget, independent film industry, appearing in some of this country's most profitable, home-grown, straight-to-DVD titles. In some respects, it's a CV most actors would be proud of. After all, acting can be a precarious and unpredictable business – just ask Lupita Nyong'o, 2013's Oscar winner for Best Supporting Actress.

In the same weekend Nyong'o picked up the Academy Award for her much-lauded, heartbreaking performance in the universally acclaimed *12 Years a Slave*, you could also catch her as air stewardess Gwen Lloyd in Liam Neeson's *Non-Stop*. With less than twenty words of dialogue, Nyong'o's character was lucky to even have a name check in the credits – she could have just as easily been billed simply as 'Stewardess number two'.

Similarly, when the panel that hosts movie magazine *Empire*'s podcast responded to a subscriber's question asking them to name an actor with a 'flawless' filmography, they struggled to come up with a single actor who could unequivocally hold their head up with pride – even the likes of Daniel Day Lewis and Michael Fassbender have on their CVs, respectively, dire musical misfire *Nine* and comic book catastrophe *Jonah Hex*.

There are two universal and obvious truths recognized in the making of movies – the first, as William Goldman, the acclaimed screenwriter of such classics as *All the President's Men*, *Misery* and *The Princess Bride* so eloquently put it in his book, *Adventures in the Screen Trade*, 'Nobody knows anything … Not one person in the entire motion picture field knows for a certainty what's going to work. Every time out it's a guess and, if you're lucky, an educated one.' The other is that actors are, almost without exception, forced to take roles they don't want because they need to keep working or the money on offer is simply too tempting to ignore.

To his credit, Danny Dyer has rarely been out of work in his twenty-year-plus career and has managed to maintain a consistently high profile – more often than not attracting unwanted attention and tabloid headlines for his behaviour off the screen rather than on it. What Dyer has achieved, and what should afford him the degree of respect he is so often denied, is his ongoing willingness to challenge people's expectations of him as well as his unfaltering determination, if largely fruitless, to be taken seriously as an actor. Most people who meet him for the first time are shocked to discover that, despite an unexpected, awkward shyness, he possesses an unmistakable old school movie-star charisma and a down-to-earth charm that completely contradicts the hard-man persona that precedes him (a persona, admittedly, that Danny has had more than a hand in perpetrating himself). In the aforementioned interview with Lovefilm.com, Danny said, 'As an actor, I don't think I've proved anything yet. I want to get a job where I don't know if I can pull it off . . . I want to think to myself each day, "Can I do this? Am I right for this?" I want that pressure; I thrive on it.'

It was with that attitude, side-stepping his initial reservations about putting himself, and his family, in the firing line, that Danny accepted the role of Mick Carter in *EastEnders*. It was obvious that the part would dramatically heighten his public profile and challenge many people's perceptions of him. While it would open him up to a new, largely untapped, fan base, in turn it might also leave him at the mercy of the increased press scrutiny that went hand in hand with being part of the soap. Danny approached his decision to take a high-profile role in one of Britain's most popular TV shows with the same instinctive certainty he had shown throughout his career – with his eyes open and confident in his own abilities. This was a man unafraid to challenge himself, put his career on the line and defy his many critics.

CHAPTER ONE

THE ARTFUL DODGER

When asked by the Sick Chirpse website in early 2013 what he thought his enduring legacy might be, Danny Dyer replied, 'I hope that I can inspire a few working class kids who are in a ghetto somewhere, with no hope, that I'm living proof that anyone can be whatever they want to be. As long as you believe in yourself and you've got talent, then you will make it.' It was with this slightly deviant attitude, while retaining a strong connection with his working-class background, that Danny managed to make something of himself, achieving a level of success and recognition most can only dream of. Danny's story is made all the more incredible when set in the context of the struggles experienced by the majority of people living in the run-down areas of East London he grew up in.

Danny Dyer was born on 24 July 1977 into a changing Britain. On the surface, things may have looked unremarkable – Liverpool FC were crowned English League champions for the tenth time, while Red Rum romped home to claim his third Grand National victory. *Star Wars*, released in the UK towards the end of that year, was about to become one of the highest grossing films of all time, while the world mourned the passing of glam-rock superstar, T.Rex's Marc Bolan, in a tragic car accident. What the outside world failed to notice, or chose to ignore, was the groundswell of social unrest and economic hardship that had hit the UK since the turn of the decade.

While most of the country may have been distracted by the extravagant celebrations taking place to commemorate the Queen's Silver Jubilee year, the working class of Britain was facing one of the bleakest economic downturns since the end of the Second World War. Job prospects were limited and reports had shown that in the three years since the 1974 general election, when the Labour government had unexpectedly snuck into power in a hung parliament, the price of the average shopping basket had risen by nearly 70 per cent and it was becoming increasingly hard to make ends meet. The country was experiencing a wave of political and social instability, with striking workers at the Leyland car manufacturing plant under threat of dismissal and the IRA terror campaign escalating as it hit the heart of London's West End. People were living under a dark cloud, gripped by fear as the Yorkshire Ripper's spate of attacks entered their second year, while youth discontentment erupted in the shape of punk – the Sex Pistols released their seminal album, *Never Mind the Bollocks, Here's the Sex Pistols* in October 1977 – and riots occurred in Birmingham following National Front marchers' clashes with anti-Nazi protesters. It's no real surprise that this was the last Labour government before a twenty-year gap that saw Thatcherism and Conservative rule last well into the 1990s.

Danny was raised on a council estate in the Custom House area in the heart of London's East End, where he lived for his entire childhood. He told the documentary *Nothing to Something*, 'It was all I knew, really. My whole family lived within streets of each other. My nan lived down the road, my uncles, my aunts, all within walking distance,' adding, 'It was a very small community.' This was not the London portrayed in the wheeler-dealer antics of lovable rogues such as *Only Fools and Horses*' Del Boy Trotter, or the frozen post-Second World War community spirit on display in *EastEnders*' fictional borough of Walford. This was a much harsher environment, and a decidedly less attractive place to live. It was the sort of breeding ground responsible for creating East London's most infamous gangsters, Reggie and Ronnie Kray, an area rife with petty crime, drowning in a festering culture of casual drug and alcohol abuse. Here, it wasn't uncommon for children to begin smoking before they'd even started primary school or to see little old ladies congregate at the local shops, their casual conversation peppered with the sort of language that might make the most foul-mouthed criminals blush. Attitudes were informed by underlying racism and homophobia, seen by most as merely a way of life: inherited, unquestioned and deeply ingrained, woven into the basic fabric of the closed communities. This prejudice, although oppressive, rarely came to the surface in any form of politically charged outburst, more often appearing as part of a petty name-calling session or, more likely, as playful, everyday pub banter.

The area had seen its fair share of adversity, having been more or less completely rebuilt after devastating bombings during the 1940 Blitz, and it was well known to be one of the most deprived areas of London. In his own autobiography, *Straight Up*, Danny acknowledges it was a tough neighbourhood to grow up in: 'Where I grew up is quite a depressing place to look at, so it's not like you could exactly lose yourself in [its] natural beauty.'

While he was born into a troubled marriage, he was never starved of attention or affection, and there was no shortage of love from his mother, two sets of surviving grandparents and an extended family. He would be the first of three children born to Antony and Christine Dyer, with a brother, Tony, and sister, Kayleigh, arriving over the course of the next few years.

His father moved out of the family home before he had turned ten years old, which shaped Danny's early life. While he admitted to Askmen.com, 'I was always out and about and had a good time as a kid … I didn't have much discipline,' he did feel he 'wasn't a bad kid'. Danny describes his father in his autobiography as a decent man who was merely a product of his circumstances, archetypal of the grafting, hard-drinking men of the time. Antony Dyer was a painter and decorator, trained by his father before him, and he worked long hours, with jobs taking him all over London and out into the suburbs. The money was acceptable, but like many men in his situation, Danny's dad was prone to spend a good proportion of his wages in the pub or out with his friends, his pay packet virtually empty before he made it home.

Although Danny says that his dad was unusual, in that he became gentler and more affectionate once he'd had a drink, it was this that caused most of the arguments between his parents before their split. However, Christine Dyer longed for a quiet life and seemed to have made her peace with the situation. But the final straw came when, shortly after the birth of Danny's sister, it was revealed Antony had been living a double life. He had started a relationship with another woman a few years earlier and had gone on to have two children with her. While the woman knew about Danny and the rest of his family, Danny's mother had been completely oblivious to her husband's infidelity. Christine was devastated and threw Antony out. Even though he was no longer living at the family home, Danny did have regular contact with his father, eventually meeting his half-siblings, but he admits this early estrangement meant he would never feel as close to his dad as he did to his mum.

While there was a predominately female influence nurturing Danny's character at home, he was also being exposed to some of the more typically masculine pursuits. Early trips to the football with his dad to see West Ham play would inspire a lifelong passion for the game and his local team.

Growing up in a tough environment, Danny was well aware that becoming a man in the East End of London was not easy. You were expected to be able to look after yourself, and with that came a certain attitude. He was also exposed to West Ham's infamous football hooligans, the ICF, and although he never became part of that culture of violence, he was aware how easy it was to be seduced by it. He recognized he was different from the more thuggish fans, admitting in his autobiography, 'I didn't have that bubbling aggression a lot of young blokes seemed to have. I was a happy-go-lucky kid – a bit scatty, a bit nutty, was always having a laugh.'

There wasn't much for children his age to do outside of school hours, aside from hanging around in a gang or watching videos at a friend's house. With money so tight (or earmarked for buying cannabis), Danny and his clique never had enough to go to the cinema, so his first experiences of seeing films would be home video copies of titles such as *Scum*, *A Clockwork Orange* and horror movies like *Salem's Lot* and *Fright Night*. While none of this feels particularly suitable for the average ten- or eleven-year-old, it was nothing compared to the library of violent videos and snuff films the boys were soon watching.

Danny was simply the result of the setting he was growing up in. Now, he likes to paint a picture of his younger self as a roguish Artful Dodger type, never getting into too much trouble, but always up for a laugh and a bit of mischief with his gang. He gave an example of one such situation to Empire Online: 'On fireworks night we used to get screamers and put 'em in scaffold poles and fire 'em at each other' – an incident that gave him a severe burn and a badly scarred leg. In an interview with the *Independent*, Danny related how he had been admitted to hospital at the age of twelve, where he had his stomach pumped after, as he puts it, 'a terrible mix' of Southern Comfort and Dr Pepper. In his autobiography he says, as a response, 'If you build a concrete jungle you can't be too surprised if you get a few monkeys swinging about in it . . . me and my mates were them monkeys.'

But the truth of the matter was a little more serious, as things had started to unravel as soon as his father left. Upset and unable to vent the frustrations he felt about his dad's betrayal and absence, he had started to bottle up his feelings. Soon, angry outbursts led to a dramatic deterioration in his behaviour. Danny admits his mother was worried enough to take him to see a counsellor, but after just a few sessions, his refusal to cooperate had led to Christine being told that there was nothing he could do for her son. Danny was also struggling at school, he told *Hunger TV* in a 2010 interview: 'It was rubbish – the only reason you went was to see a fight after [classes] . . . In science and maths, the boffin kids would be cracking on, when for me it was like Arabic.'

He started to smoke cannabis, and the 'mucking about' soon led to petty theft. He and his gang would steal from the back of parked Parcelforce vans or take bikes while their owners were looking the other way. They would sell their loot for small change in order to get enough money for drugs. Although it looked like Danny was getting sucked into a pattern of escalating crime and drug use, he reasoned in his book, 'Anything you do in life you need to get a buzz out of, and it just didn't happen for me when we were on the rob . . . I never got a thrill from it.' Reassuringly, he finished, 'I don't really think crime was for me . . . I got more of a buzz out of the fact that I'd be getting some puff later on.'

With Danny's behaviour becoming more difficult to manage, he moved to his local secondary school, Woodside Comprehensive. With little or no interest in the standard academic subjects, he recalled in *Straight Up*, 'Maths, English, science, I just couldn't understand any of them . . . It was just a case of f*****g around in lessons and being silly until I got kicked out at sixteen.' He was resigned to his fate, contemplating entering the painting and decorating trade alongside his father. 'I couldn't see any future for myself other than doing what my dad did – going to work, hating it, coming home, getting p****d, going to sleep, repeat until retirement or death.' But something extraordinary was about to happen. On what Danny assumed would be a typically boring Tuesday afternoon of lessons, on only his second day at high school, he attended his first drama class. Without exaggeration, it changed his life forever.

The experience was a revelation for Danny. He told *Hunger TV*: 'When I walked in the drama lesson, it just felt so natural. I looked around the class and couldn't understand why no one else could do it.' In his autobiography, *Straight Up*, he recalled that, 'I'd never done any nativity plays at junior school, never done any acting before ... [but] I knew I was good at it, much better than anyone else in the class.' He took to it like a duck to water, thriving while others floundered self-consciously. He never felt nervous or awkward about getting up and performing in front of the rest of the class, although he had to keep the acting classes secret from most of his mates, as he told the *Independent*. 'Drama was a girls' thing. I lied to people when they asked where I was going. It was a secret pleasure.'

Secret or not, Danny had finally found a subject that he enjoyed. He was a natural show-off who craved attention, but more than that, he was experiencing the elation of being really good at something and had found an outlet for all the pent-up frustration and aggression he had been carrying since his dad left home. He started to use his emotions and experiences in the class and it helped him effortlessly create different characters. The only downside was returning to normal lessons.

He wanted more and vowed to keep feeding his newfound hunger. Despite having to mix with kids outside his normal group, he joined an after-school drama club, and here he excelled. Showing much more promise than the other students, Danny had the full support of the drama teacher, Miss Flynn, who encouraged him to take this new hobby seriously.

Danny loved the classes but when it came to choosing his exam subjects, he was mindful of his future job prospects and worried that acting might be a dead end. Danny liked art and wondered if it might offer him a more secure future. But Miss Flynn was adamant Danny needed to stick with drama. He recalls how passionate she was, telling *Hunger TV*, 'In moments when I was a bit of a pr*ck, she would pull me aside and tell me straight: "Look, you're really talented, you should think about this as a career."'

Danny would eventually get a B in his drama course – an amazing achievement for a student not enamoured of academic pursuits, even if he does admit most of the written coursework was actually completed by his brother Tony!

With Miss Flynn's continued support, Danny started to attend another after-school drama club, at nearby Star Lane.

Here he would have the chance to take part in bigger, more professional productions, and at last let his mum see him perform in a proper play. But it was an opportunity that came with its own price and a degree of risk to Danny's personal safety. Star Lane school was situated in Canning Town, and the children who lived there were bitter rivals to Danny's Custom House gang. His mischievous exploits meant he had become a well-known face in neighbouring territories and any rival gangs would relish the chance to catch him on their turf. In the end, Danny couldn't resist this new challenge and crossed enemy lines. He reflected in his autobiography that 'It was worth it. The love of drama made me take that risk of a beating and of ridicule. It was fantastic.' His sense of pride and achievement fuelled his need to learn and accomplish even more.

The drama group wasn't Danny's only new discovery upon moving to secondary school. He had started to take a lot more notice of the girls there, and one girl in particular caught Danny's attention: Joanne Mas. Joanne was almost the complete opposite of Danny – she was well behaved, attentive in class and well liked by the teachers. She enjoyed most of her school subjects and showed great potential in many of them. She was a very pretty girl, her father's Spanish heritage giving her an exotic quality, which made her stand out from the crowd. She was the girl everyone fancied. Danny couldn't believe his luck when Joanne made it clear she was interested in him, too. Their first date – which Joanne paid for – was a respectable affair, a sit-down meal in a proper pizza restaurant, rather than the local fast-food establishment many might have expected. As things progressed, Danny realized this was something special; there was a connection present that he had never felt before.

Joanne quickly became a constant in Danny's life, and,

although her parents were initially sceptical about him – he did, after all, come from a broken family and was a well-known troublemaker in the area – they accepted Danny was more than just a passing teenage crush and welcomed him into their home.

At the same time as his relationship with Joanne was developing, Danny's acting was also going from strength to strength. It was becoming very clear that this was much more than just a hobby for him, and the teachers at both drama groups he attended agreed he was showing the kind of potential worthy of more intensive nurturing. Well aware he wasn't going to have the financial support available to typical stage school children, they managed to track down a drama programme specifically set up to help under-privileged youngsters, kids from single-parent families or anyone who might struggle to pay drama school fees. Danny was leaving his East London stomping ground and heading north, to Kentish Town, to a weekend drama group at the Interchange Studios.

While appearing as a guest on the BBC's *The One Show* in 2014, Danny was teased by the hosts, Chris Evans and Fearne Cotton, about a mystery guest from his past who had been drafted in to keep him under control and who he 'wouldn't want to get on the wrong side of'. While Danny was visibly confused, perhaps imagining Vinnie Jones or some 'kiss-and-tell' figure from his past, they eventually surprised him, live on air, with a beaming and emotional Miss Flynn, his first drama teacher. A shocked Danny exclaimed, before embracing his old teacher, 'No way . . . I can't believe it.' Having not seen Danny in person for over twenty years, Miss Flynn reaffirmed her early faith in him, bursting with pride as she revealed, 'He was so talented, he was very special . . . so committed to his acting.' She knowingly added, 'He was mischievous, he was a real pain at school, but in his drama lessons he was fab, absolutely fab.' Danny was clearly moved, and, choking on his words, asked, 'Where'd you find her? She always believed in me, there wasn't many that did . . . she was a real support.'

Clearly, Danny would never forget the 'beyond the call of duty' approach employed by his early supporters, or the endless words of encouragement given to him by Miss Flynn. It would stay with him throughout his career and he gratefully acknowledged her outstanding contribution in *Straight Up*, his 2010 autobiography, relating that before he met her he had never thought of acting as something he could do as a viable job. Danny confessed that shortly after she introduced him to the drama class, he was hooked: 'It was like a drug to me. I couldn't get enough.' Thankfully this addiction, rather than many others he was soon to encounter, would be the passion that shaped the rest of his life.

CHAPTER TWO

INTERCHANGE

It was with some trepidation that Danny embarked upon the next stage of his acting dream. These would not be enforced school drama lessons; everyone entering the Interchange had been recommended to apply because they had already displayed promise and had been confirmed as having talent. More importantly, they wanted to be there. Danny was no longer the one bright spark among a bunch of kids 'mucking around' to keep themselves busy. Nevertheless, it came as no surprise to him or Miss Flynn that he excelled during the selection process and was accepted into the programme immediately. Danny was entering an exclusive world that had until now seemed far out of reach.

Celia Greenwood was a founder and leading light in the Interchange. Initially based in Kentish Town, the organization had been forced to relocate to its present home in North London's Hampstead Town Hall after its original premises were sold to developers and demolished. Now under the name WAC Arts, it continued to evolve and expand and still flourishes some thirty-five years after its conception. Greenwood told the AND (A New Direction for Arts) website: 'A colleague and I were aware that we were working with a lot of young people who had enormous capacity to become employed within the creative industries but were never going to get there – because they did not have whatever it was to compete on an equal playing field with kids who had ballet lessons from the age of five.' She recognized school drama classes and after-school clubs, like the ones Danny had attended, were a good starting point, but little more than a foundation.

The Interchange Studios had been set up as a real alternative to established drama courses and stage schools. It was a charitable body, but its aim was to give disadvantaged children the same standard of training as their more privileged peers. It offered classes that were grounded in the basics, with a focus on the more practical aspects of the profession. It also gave its graduates a solid base in the technical and creative skills required to flourish in the performing arts.

What started as a Sunday club, and then later expanded to offer full weekend classes, would eventually grow into a hugely successful education programme. For Danny, this new experience fanned the flames of his acting obsession, opening his eyes to a wealth of previously unimaginable opportunities and areas of his craft, such as singing, dance and even mime. Although it quickly became clear Danny was not going to be joining the cast of *Les Misérables* or *Billy Elliot*, he did enrol in the course that concentrated specifically on drama and acting technique. Even at this stage Danny understood that learning the basics would prove useful.

Interchange's survival relied on the generous donations of time and resources from full-time actors, which meant the students had the chance to mingle with people who were in professional productions, appearing on television and making a living from acting. Danny was seeing, first hand, what it would be like to choose acting as a serious career option.

Interchange had gained a reputation as a genuine hotbed of talent and had quickly become a magnet for casting directors and agents looking to either fill a specific role or simply swell their rosters with fresh faces. The studio held special workshops for these agents, allowing them to come and see the kids in action, showcasing the ones they thought displayed the most promise. It was during one of these workshops that Danny was spotted by Charlotte Kelly. Kelly was an established agent and she had come to Interchange looking for a more rough-and-ready actor than the average stage school graduate, but it was clear she saw greater potential in Danny than in just filling one specific role.

Danny relished every opportunity and, even at this early stage, had an easy charm and a relatable quality that set him apart. In *Straight Up*, he suggests Kelly could sense he was serious about developing his talent: 'People could see I wasn't in it for money or fame or anything like that, they could see I just loved it, was good at it and wanted to absorb and learn more.' Danny describes his first meeting with Kelly, saying, 'I didn't know it but, as she smiled at me and went to shake my hand, my life changed big style.' He continued, 'We were introduced and she said, "I think you're incredibly talented and I'd like to represent you. This is quite a rare thing for me as an agent because I haven't got child actors on my books."'

She asked him if he had thought seriously about acting as a career, and if he was interested, she could set him up with an audition for a part the very next day. Danny couldn't believe his luck, and was even more shocked when she told him it was for a part in the latest instalment of police drama series *Prime Suspect*. This was a dream come true, and much more than anyone could have hoped for from their first real audition. This wasn't for just a day working as an extra or playing 'boy outside shop' in a walk-on part, this was for a speaking part in a high-profile TV show. As he says in true

Danny fashion in *Straight Up*, he was 'well up for it'.

Danny couldn't wait to get home to tell his mum, brandishing the business card Kelly had given him. The audition was arranged for the next day, and in an act of typical independence, Danny travelled into central London to the Soho offices where the audition was taking place on his own. Central London was relatively unfamiliar territory for the fourteen-year-old Danny, but he was determined to do this solo. As he explained in his autobiography, 'I went on my jack . . . this has always been a very personal thing for me, it's something I've always done off my own back. I've never had a leg up.' There were a couple of other kids in the waiting room, accompanied by their mums or dads, but Danny could already tell he was going to hit this one out of the park.

The casting agent was Doreen Jones, and as soon as Danny walked into the room, she knew he was the real deal. The role was to play Martin Fletcher, a homeless, glue-sniffing rent boy and Danny, with his long greasy hair and scruffy clothes, looked like he understood some of the hardships a kid like Martin had gone through. He recalled, 'I had the edge . . . it's about the performance . . . The reason I'm there is to show them I'm better than anyone else for this part. It's not about whether I'm articulate or dressed the right way.' It worked: Danny was offered the role before the end of the day. He was about to do his first job as a professional actor opposite Helen Mirren – a boy, let us not forget, who had never even been in a school play. Danny was on his way.

When the first run of *Prime Suspect*, starring Helen Mirren, was aired on ITV in 1991, it had been a critical and commercial hit, with a second series enjoying similar success. This would be the third installment, the action moving to the seedy underworld of London's Soho with Mirren's character, Jane

Tennison, now working for the vice squad as she investigates a cover-up involving police corruption, underage rent boys, blackmail and murder. It would prove to be a real high point for Mirren and the series, launching the careers of not only Danny, but also Jonny Lee Miller, several years ahead of his breakout performance in Danny Boyle's *Trainspotting*. Also featured were David Thewlis as a vindictive pimp, James Jackson and a turn from future *Doctor Who* star, Peter Capaldi, as a transvestite torch-singer.

Although set in London, most of the filming would take place in Manchester. This meant Danny had to travel north for the five days allocated for filming his scenes and stay in a hotel near to the production's sets and outdoor locations. Back then, this was the farthest Danny had ever travelled away from home and it was his first time he'd ever stayed in a hotel. Being a minor, Danny needed a chaperon and as this was a paid job (he received £50 a day), it seemed a good way for him to make sure his mother would get something out of it, too. She would accompany him to Manchester for the first couple of days but, as she couldn't leave Danny's brother and sister for too long, his father would take over for the rest of the shoot. Danny's first experiences on set were some of the most valuable lessons he would ever learn.

He got his first taste of method acting when David Thewlis would blank him on and off set. The unease he felt around the actor heightened the tension in front of the camera and their scenes together were especially powerful as you can see the genuine fear and distrust in Danny's performance.

The debutant felt completely at home on the production. He was fascinated by the chaos and mayhem. In the many hours all actors spend on set waiting between scenes, he would be eavesdropping on what the cameramen were saying, grabbing titbits of advice from the other actors and feeding off the buzz from the whole crew. He recalls how it felt in his book: 'The whole process was magical to me . . . I'd found my calling.' He had to pinch himself: 'This is me just doing what I do and there's people paying me to be here. Ridiculous.'

Danny's biggest challenge would be his scenes with Helen Mirren. Although she was already a well-respected stage and screen presence before *Prime Suspect*, the show really had turned Mirren into a household name and remains one of her best-known roles. She was a force to be reckoned with on set, but she was keen to put Danny at ease, well aware it was his first big job. She spent some time with his father and him before filming began on their scenes, prompting him to admit in an interview with *The Lady* magazine more than twenty years later, 'My dad was more star struck than I was ... I was a total hormonal teenage boy and I was just bang in love with her.' Danny explained how Mirren made a concerted effort to gain his trust and to look out for him, saying, 'She really helped me along and guided me through it.' Danny left the *Prime Suspect* set with nothing but praise for his first leading lady, describing her as a 'beautiful, beautiful, elegant woman', and his respect and admiration for her has never faded.

Prime Suspect had been a magical experience for Danny on so many levels and, with little concession to the fact it was his first time in front of the camera, he delivered a confident and compelling performance he can still be proud of. His portrayal of Martin Fletcher is rooted in a gritty truth that would have been lost with a more polished, experienced child actor. Danny looks younger than his fourteen years, giving the character a heartbreaking vulnerability despite the streetwise, cocky bravado on display, and this ultimately injects some real emotional clout to the inevitability of Martin's tragic fate.

Prime Suspect 3 would win numerous awards including two BAFTAs (for Best Drama Series and Best TV Actress for Mirren) and picked up the Emmy Award for Outstanding Miniseries when it was shown in the US in early 1994. It was an amazing first step into the acting industry for Danny and proved to be a solid launch pad for his fledgling career.

His only regret about his *Prime Suspect* experience was the fact the show took so long to air, not hitting UK television screens until the end of December 1993, when Danny was sixteen. Sadly, his granddad, who had been ill for a while, died before he could see his grandson in action.

It was at around the same time he'd got the *Prime Suspect* audition that Danny's mother announced her dad had been diagnosed with prostate cancer. She suggested the best thing would be if Danny moved into his granddad's house to help look after him and his nan. He agreed, and although he found it hard, he was there for both his grandparents, watching his grandfather grow weaker and more helpless as the illness took its toll. Almost a year later, Danny's granddad was moved to hospital where he eventually passed away.

Danny took his death very hard. He admits that it was around this time he started to dabble in harder drugs alongside his long-time cannabis habit. In his autobiography, he relates how it was the easiest way to escape and numb the grief he was feeling. 'It wasn't a happy time and I wanted to forget about it so I'd just take a load of drugs and f**k off out of the house, lose myself hanging around with my mates.' Danny has always been fairly candid about his use of drugs, admitting that in later life he found himself wrestling with demons he recognized as having roots in the more traumatic periods of his late teens.

It's easy to speculate that the pressure and grief he was

experiencing could have been the start of a catastrophic downward spiral for Danny – so many children his age and in his situation end up trapped in a vicious cycle of drugs and crime. Thankfully, Danny had his fledgling career to concentrate on and, although on the surface they may have seemed dysfunctional, he had the full support of his extended family.

As he entered his late teens, Danny was travelling up and down the country to auditions and landed countless acting jobs in a variety of interesting roles, several taking him to some pretty far-flung locations, including trips to Budapest and Ireland. Over the next few years he would appear in some of British television's most popular and high-profile shows, including *A Touch of Frost, Cadfael, The Bill* and *Soldier Soldier*. Of course, Danny had another stabilizing constant in his life – Joanne – and their relationship would soon take off in a completely new, unexpected direction.

Danny never forgot how important the Interchange had been in giving him a solid starting point and the focus he needed to succeed. It was because of the encouragement and selfless nurturing he received there that he was able to realize his dream and consider acting as a full-time profession. Danny maintained links with the organization throughout his career and when funding was reduced or cutbacks threatened to close the initiative for good, he would always be there to offer his time and support at various events.

CHAPTER THREE

BABY LOVE

After completing his work on *Prime Suspect*, Danny's world seemed a much bigger and more exciting place. He was now a real actor, with a proper agent, and he was determined not to look back. From the minute he signed with Charlotte Kelly, Danny was regularly attending auditions and enjoyed a commendably high success rate for an untrained newcomer, being offered virtually everything he went up for. It wasn't long before he had a relatively good, steady income for someone his age. He began to be recognized around the estate where he grew up and still lived, and received letters from fans in the US after *Prime Suspect* aired there in early 1994. There was no time to rest on his laurels and bask in past glories, however, and Danny was only too aware of the old adage, 'You're only as good as your last job' – he was resolute in his desire not to let the grass grow under his feet.

On *Cadfael*, his next proper job, he worked alongside Derek Jacobi and, although Danny had a natural flair for acting, he was mindful he still had a lot to learn. The rehearsal rooms and film sets became his classroom and he spent most of his downtime on location talking to the crew and other actors, quizzing them about their experiences and the industry, taking every opportunity to soak up the knowledge and wealth of experience available to him. Danny was also meeting actors of a similar age, and although he knew he could match them on set, he struggled to find much in common with them off set. He would discover that there were only a few people who shared his background on the average production, and most of them stood behind the cameras. Danny was finding out the hard way just how unusual he was: virtually every other actor he worked with had come from traditional stage schools or drama colleges and he felt compelled to prove he was just as good as they were.

In 1995, Danny met another young actor called Craig Kelly. He had come to Danny's attention when Kelly starred alongside Harvey Keitel in *The Young Americans*, the high-profile British gangster film directed by Danny Cannon (British co-creator of the hugely successful *CSI* franchise). The film had been a commercial and critical success and many assumed it would be the springboard that would launch Kelly's career in America. Danny was more than a little surprised to find himself acting in an episode of *A Touch of Frost* alongside someone he'd seen as a real rising star only a couple of years earlier.

Whether he realized it or not, Danny was getting some harsh but valuable lessons about the fickle nature of fame and the acting profession. In *Straight Up*, Danny recalls the instruction Kelly gave him – 'Whatever happens, don't get too big for your f*****g boots, boy.' Kelly explained, 'People kept telling me to turn everything down. I went through a period of six months saying, "Won't do that, won't do that" and I missed the boat over there.' It would be a story Danny would never forget and a philosophy, in terms of his career, that he has steadfastly stuck to – indeed, some would suggest he took this advice too much to heart in recent years and should have said 'no' a few more times than he did.

Danny's career took a few unexpected turns as he was

encouraged to audition for stage plays as well as television and film work. He auditioned for a play that was to be directed by Alan Rickman, and although he didn't get the part, he received a personal note from Rickman explaining his rejection and encouraging him to keep working. On receiving the letter, Danny immediately wrote back and invited Rickman to see him perform in a play he was appearing in at the time, *Not Gods But Giants*. To his astonishment, Rickman accepted his invitation. He attended a showing, laughed heartily throughout and spent time with Danny and the rest of cast after the show. Danny was struck by how good this simple act of kindness had made him feel and vowed never to forget it.

Not Gods But Giants transferred to the Edinburgh International Festival that year, but Danny was unable to follow as he'd secured a decent part in a BBC drama, due to start filming in Dublin before the end of the play's run. *Loving* was set during the Second World War and focused on the lives and loves of the servants working in a remote stately home. Having recently turned eighteen, this would be Danny's first time working away from home without needing a chaperon and it would prove to be another steep learning curve.

Danny relished the opportunity to study older and more experienced actors, his competitive nature continually asserting itself in his will to be as good as them. What he found difficult was the time they would have to spend together outside of work. It could be a fairly intense situation – spending twenty-four hours a day, sometimes for weeks on end, living on top of each other with people you barely knew and had little, or nothing, in common with. Instead of letting the situation affect him, Danny used his isolation and awkwardness in his performance. He started to collect these strong feelings – such as the grief he'd felt when his beloved childhood dog, Sam, died – quelling every emotion until he needed them during the scene. He would then reach deep inside of himself and drag everything to the surface for the take. In *Loving*, his character, Bert, is involved in a doomed romantic triangle, and at one point is left devastated and sobs uncontrollably. Danny gave an outstanding performance, showing a much softer, less cocksure side of himself, stretching his limits as an actor and demonstrating he had more than one string to his bow.

Among the other cast members was Mark Rylance, and Danny savoured the chance to work alongside a man who would become a lifelong inspiration and acting hero. Danny insists in his book that his experience working with Rylance was worth its weight in gold, saying, 'I didn't need to go to drama school because I worked with someone on *Loving* who has been my drama school.' Rylance was the polar opposite in terms of the method extremes of the likes of David Thewlis, whom Danny had watched alienate his fellow cast members on *Prime Suspect*. Danny marvelled at Rylance's ability to appear fully immersed in a scene, break to share a joke or laugh with his young co-star, only to then switch instantly back into character when required. Danny's eyes were being opened to the unlimited possibilities of his newly chosen profession, just as a cruel inevitability was about to throw a huge spanner in the works.

Danny was undeniably young-looking for his age (as used to great effect in *Prime Suspect*), not hitting puberty until well into his mid-teens, but, as he turned eighteen in 1995, his appearance began to change more dramatically and he could no longer pitch for the boyish roles he had once so successfully portrayed. As a child actor, Danny had been a big fish in a small pond, his raw intensity being a unique selling point, rewarding him with a virtually unbroken success rate at auditions. As a young man, Danny was now competing in a much more crowded, much more ruthless arena. The phone rang less frequently and when it did, there was no longer any guarantee Danny would walk away with a job after every audition. As if that wasn't enough, Danny was about to receive some more life-changing news: he was about to become a father for the first time.

Danny and Joanne had been inseparable since they met a few years earlier. Although Joanne's parents were quite protective and either did not know, or quietly accepted, the full extent of their daughter's relationship with Danny, the couple had been sleeping together at his house. Danny had had other girlfriends before Joanne, but this was different. The couple shared a decidedly more intense and mature connection.

While they were more or less the same age, Joanne had a much more sensible approach to sex than Danny and had started taking the pill as soon as their relationship turned more physical. It came as a bit of a shock, then, when Joanne took Danny aside one evening and told him that she was pregnant. As far as Joanne was concerned, she was determined she was going to keep the baby. She told Danny she would accept the fact he might not want to stand by her and help raise the child, and didn't want to put any pressure on him. Joanne understood that they were both very young, Danny's career was already in flux, and with the added complication of bringing up a baby, it might all be too much of a distraction during this period of transition.

Danny told Askmen.com, 'There is never a right or wrong time to have kids . . . you can have this paranoia, "Will I be able to do this? I'm not sure if I'm ready to have kids."' He added, 'As long as you're loved up and soul mates with the person you have them with, then you'll be fine.' Knowing Joanne was definitely the person he wanted to be with for the rest of his life, he decided he needed to do everything in his power to help provide for their baby and he made one of the toughest decisions of his life: he wasn't going to sit around waiting for the phone to ring anymore, he was going to have to take on a 'proper' job and start bringing in regular money.

So began a period where Danny had to put his acting ambitions on hold. He couldn't bear to think his dream was actually over, he just knew in the short term it had to come second to Joanne, the new baby and earning enough money to survive. He joined his father on some painting and decorating jobs. He was grateful, even if Antony never let him actually touch a paint brush, resigning him to the sweeping up and fetching and carrying. But when that dried up, Danny had to turn to temporary labouring jobs. He hated it. He had been given a taste of something he loved, something he was good at and it was a crushing blow to feel it slip away.

Danny and Joanne moved into a small flat around the time the baby was born in August 1996. They named their little girl Dani, and she was instantly the apple of her dad's eye. Money was tight and the couple struggled to make ends meet, but Danny was adamant that acting was his best chance to offer his new family a better life. He was still trying to attend as many auditions as possible, but his success rate had dropped dramatically and he was finding it increasingly hard to be seen even for the parts he knew he would be good for. He grew bitter, watching other people playing the roles he had been rejected for and it triggered a relapse of the anger problems he'd experienced in his early teens, straining his relationship with Joanne. It fed his hunger, though, and Danny started to channel that aggression in his auditions. In his autobiography he explains how he would look at the other candidates in the room, all going up for the same part, and think, 'You're going to take the food out of my baby's mouth', and it would start the adrenaline pumping. While it didn't work for every part, there was no mistaking Danny's passion and the fire that burned inside him.

As luck would have it, a similarly driven young writer and director, Justin Kerrigan, was working on a script he hoped would speak to Danny's discontented generation. His aim was to tap into a growing underground club culture that was spreading fast in 1990s Britain. He believed his film, *Human Traffic*, could create an unstoppable chemical reaction among like-minded groups of partygoers fuelled in equal measure by their rage and passion, their rejection of the mundane nine-to-five, their unbreakable friendships and their almost instinctive need to 'blow their minds' in clubs and bars the length and breadth of the country. And there was a perfect part in it for Danny.

CHAPTER FOUR

HIGHER THAN THE SUN

When asked by the *Guardian* in 2013 how much research Danny had had to do in order to convincingly play Moff, the pilled-up, motor-mouthed cockney he'd brought so vividly to life in *Human Traffic*, he said, 'That role was me – I was still living it then.' He reiterated this in an interview with Jonathan Sothcott and James Mullinger for their book, *The Films of Danny Dyer*: 'The partying, the joy and the ecstasy [the world of *Human Traffic*] was basically the world that I was living in at the time.' Evidently, Danny had a few more responsibilities than the young, free and single Moff back in 1997, but he was certainly enjoying more of a party lifestyle than the average new dad – his first daughter, Dani, having arrived only a year or so earlier.

He admits he wasn't in a great place when he received the *Human Traffic* script, with offers of acting work having more or less dried up. While Danny had never really considered giving up forever, there was a massive gulf between what he wanted to do and what he had to do to keep money coming in. There was a crushing irony in the fact that he was finding it so hard to find work just when his need to be earning had never been more vital. He found it virtually impossible to juggle auditions with holding down any sort of normal job and their gruelling nature was taking its toll on him. So when he received the *Human Traffic* script – depicting the lives of a gang of twentysomethings who bond over their shared hatred of nine-to-five drudgery and all-consuming passions for music, drugs and clubbing – Danny knew the film could be his lifeline. He was blown away by how much he related to these characters, stating in his book, 'It excited me so much because it was basically a description of my life.' He continued, 'That life was all around me. I could see my mates living it, I was living it, everyone I knew was living it.' He acknowledges how close he'd come to throwing in the towel and admitting it was 'game over', confessing, 'I read the script virtually drooling. I thought, "This is the final straw for me. If I don't get this job then I'm not bothering no more. I can't stand the rejection."'

It's clear that Danny was focused and passionate about this project, convinced a role in the film could kick-start phase two of his acting career. The best part of a year of not working in the industry had made Danny realize that, in order to bring in the necessary funds, he needed to progress his career to the next level. Even if the phone had been ringing off the hook, he was aware that poorly paid stage roles and one-off parts in television dramas were not going to be enough. *Human Traffic* could well be his last chance to break out of the minor leagues and finally get into feature films.

In the 1990s, Britain had undergone a mini-revolution. Club culture had gripped the night-time scene, breaking free of its underground shackles to become a genuine youth phenomenon. Powered by an influx of cheap 'party drugs', chiefly ecstasy, an era of dance music and clubbing was born. The rock-dance hybrid, block-rockin' beats of The Chemical Brothers, superstar DJs such as Fatboy Slim and an explosion of euphoric electronic dance music soundtracked the scene, which was bigger and more inclusive than ever before. Taking ecstasy tablets on a night out had become the norm for a number of Britain's partygoers – not only was it readily available and a much cheaper alternative to a night spent drinking alcohol, it fitted seamlessly with the music and the lifestyle of this 'living for the weekend' generation. The high was controlled – it could be timed to lift you as soon as you hit the dance floor – and the side effects, it seemed at the time, were minimal. You could leave work on Friday, party through Saturday, relax on Sunday and return to work on Monday morning with little threat of the crushing hangover associated with a similarly debauched, alcohol-fuelled weekend. People were living this way week in, week out. It had become a sustainable way of life for many; recreational rather than something they depended upon, unlikely to send them on a downward spiral into harder drugs and self-destructive addiction.

In 1996, Danny Boyle's film adaptation of Irvine Welsh's novel, *Trainspotting*, picked up on this latter theme, and had been a runaway box-office hit in UK cinemas, becoming the highest grossing British film of the year and thrusting Boyle, as well as most of the film's cast, onto the international stage. In *The Films of Danny Dyer*, Danny recalls, '*Trainspotting* had been out, and I remember being fascinated by that film and just how raw it was.' Yet he didn't relate to the lives of the film's main characters, strung out on heroine and out of control: 'Of course the idea of smack and the dark, underground, weird world that these smackheads live in was fascinating, but I'm not part of that.' Luckily for Danny, someone else was similarly inspired by Boyle's frank and unfiltered view of the state of modern Britain.

Justin Kerrigan had just turned twenty-five when he began on *Human Traffic*, his feature film debut, and he was determined the film would be a true insight into a world he knew well. He hoped it would reflect not only what was going on in his Cardiff hometown, but in virtually every city, town and village across the country. He told *Guardian* journalist Mark Morris, at the time of the film's release, 'We're talking about a massive mainstream youth culture. It's the biggest youth culture in the history of Britain [and] we don't have any filmic representation of it.' Everyone in Kerrigan's script was an extension of his own personality – he literally *was* all of the characters. While impressed by *Trainspotting*, Kerrigan's main aim was to avoid the browbeating and moral judgement running through Boyle's film. As Peter Bradshaw commented in his *Guardian* review at the time, 'No one gets to climb out of a lavatory; there are no crisis scenes … They do drugs; they have a fantastic time; that's it.'

Danny recalls in his interview with Sothcott and Mullinger that it was this uncomplicated and previously undocumented truth that grabbed his attention: '[It was great] to read something so honest, so brutally honest, with no moral ending. It is just about a group of people going out [and] getting f****d up. They've got s**t jobs, getting off their nut, bit of a comedown, roll credits. I just thought that was so great, I'd never read anything like it.' He appreciated that the script 'was stating the fact that millions of people take drugs, and they take drugs because they want to, and the majority of people have a f*****g good time'.

For Danny, the stakes going into his *Human Traffic* audition were probably the highest he would ever face in his professional life: it was for his first film, he was desperate for work and failure may have seen him quit acting for good. He knew he could play this character, he knew Moff, he had lived Moff; he was sure he could pull it off. In the end, the audition turned out to be the nearest thing to a certainty that Danny would ever experience. He recalled in an interview with the *Guardian*: 'That audition is the only one I ever had where the first question was, "Do you take drugs?" I said, "Yes, I love drugs." They were like, "Perfect."'

Kerrigan's insistence that his actors needed to have experienced drugs to fully understand the world the characters inhabited meant he would scare off a few established actors nervous about controversy or a tabloid backlash. Back then, as much as today, controversy was not something that worried Danny. He had very little to lose in terms of his professional reputation, and he had it all to gain in making the biggest splash possible with his first major screen role. He was on song during the reading, and even managed to persuade Kerrigan he would be better playing Moff in his own accent, rather than attempting the Welsh accent in the script. Kerrigan hired Danny and rewrote the character to explain Moff's displacement from London to Cardiff.

The filming took place mostly in Cardiff, and the set became the hub for an extended, six-week party. Danny became so fully immersed in the character, insisting authenticity was key to his performance, that he was more or less living as Moff for the entire shoot. His time away from home was, for him, a welcome break from the pressures and routines of family life, but for Joanne it couldn't have been so easy. Danny admits he cut himself off from reality while on location. Cardiff was, as it is now, a buzzing party town, acting as a major distraction and an oasis of pleasure to the surrounding towns and villages, and the crew took full advantage of what was on offer. What ensued was six weeks of debauchery, with Danny not paying much attention to his spending or worrying about what was going on with his young family back in London.

The extremely tight budget on the picture meant the

script was constantly changing in order to accommodate compromises of scale and cuts enforced by the film's producers and financial backers. Everyone involved was working hard, but they were also playing hard. Danny told Sothcott and Mullinger, 'In all honesty, I owed them money by the end of the job … I'd [spent] all my wages.' It was unlikely Joanne saw the funny side when Danny eventually returned home from Cardiff with little to show for his time away.

John Simm could be considered the star of the film – he was red-hot after a memorable turn in *Cracker* and his first lead role in the BBC's *The Lakes* – but in truth the film was a real ensemble piece, with each of the main cast enjoying some unforgettable moments. As filming started, Danny was proving to be a big hit with the creative team. He explained in *The Films of Danny Dyer*, 'I had the best part and I knew that, and I knew that when I got it, so I just knew that I had to work hard.' Danny illustrated this in his film-stealing scene as a passenger in a cab, manic and off his face on speed, talking about the film *Taxi Driver* to his driver. It was in this scene a movie star was born.

Human Traffic was a real education for Danny – a catalogue of firsts, and none more memorable than his first sex scene … well, almost. In one classic sequence, Moff is caught masturbating by his mother as she enters his bedroom without him realizing. It was an experience he would never forget. On seeing the final scene in the cinema, in the presence of his mum and grandma, he joked in his autobiography, 'I've had more comfortable evenings at the cinema, let me tell you.'

Joanne travelled to Cardiff to join Danny for the last couple of days on set. He neglected to mention what had happened to the £3,000 he had been paid for the job until they got home, as he was afraid to tell Joanne it had more or less covered his bar bill at the hotel. Joanne was understandably upset and Danny returned to London in a slightly worse financial shape than when he left. But he knew he had played his part in making something special and could claim a large proportion of the credit for the film's eventual success. He said in *The Films of Danny Dyer*, 'I was proud of my performance. I really felt I stood out ... I was just proud to be in it, because I knew that if this movie had come out and I hadn't been in it, it would have been a film I'd love to have seen.'

The road to the film's completion and release was a long and fraught one. Wrangles with the producers and months of re-recording lost dialogue meant the film didn't hit UK cinemas until almost two years after wrapping principal photography. Much of the tabloid controversy that then followed the film's release in 1999 was directed at the seemingly carefree and ubiquitous drug use in the film. Although there are no scenes of anyone actually taking drugs, the implied actions of the characters seemed irresponsible and reckless to anyone over a certain age and, apparently, the average broadsheet film reviewer. At the time, Kerrigan defended the film in the *Guardian*: 'If the film's controversial, that means that life's controversial.' Danny was quoted in the same article as saying, 'A lot of people ain't going to like it. If they want to do a live debate programme on it, I'm prepared to go on. This film shows the way it is, every weekend.' Perhaps, considering the trouble Danny's opinions and unedited comments have since got him into, it's just as well this televised debate never happened. Yet the film did cause discussion and put casual drug use, particularly ecstasy, into a number of tabloid headlines and, subsequently, onto several political agendas.

Like *Trainspotting* before it, the film touched a nerve with its intended audience and became a reasonable box office success, making nearly £2.5 million in the UK and later becoming a big DVD seller. Danny looks back on *Human Traffic* fondly in Sothcott and Mullinger's book, recognizing its importance in his career. 'I think that a lot of people have forgotten about *Human Traffic* . . . [but] it still has got its cult following . . . I always love it when people do come up and talk about *Human Traffic*, but it is a rare thing.' He concluded, 'I think it made people stand up and pay attention to me . . . I was young . . . It was the start of my journey, so it's always going to be close to my heart.' In true Danny Dyer fashion, he joked, 'It was certainly a good way of telling my parents that I take drugs.'

Danny's wait for his next movie job was agonizingly long. Despite knowing he had done good work on *Human Traffic*, the film would not be seen by anyone inside or outside the industry for some time. Danny returned to labouring work, but with a new confidence and now fully assured, after his experience on the film, that it was just a matter of time before he would be working full time as an actor again. He kept in practice by taking stage work, but as soon as the buzz started to build about his performance in *Human Traffic*, the phone started ringing again. He would soon work with some of the most talented directors and writers in British independent cinema, be offered a variety of unexpected and challenging roles and enjoy an eclectic start to his film career.

Danny's next film, *The Trench*, was the directorial debut of the acclaimed best-selling novelist, William Boyd, and brought together another young and inexperienced ensemble cast. The main character was portrayed by Paul Nicholls, who had come to fame playing Joe Wicks in *EastEnders*, and was now reaping the rewards of leaving the show on a high. However, he struggled to cope with the fame and unwanted paparazzi attention and disliked the 'teen pin-up' status thrust upon him by his exposure on the soap, and was looking for a change of scene.

Like Danny, Nicholls was a working-class kid from a single-parent family, having grown up in Bolton in the north of England, and came to acting after showing exceptional promise at a young age. The pair had plenty in common and bonded quickly on *The Trench*'s set. Danny was a couple of years older than Paul, but as a relative unknown at this stage, he could only imagine the pressures his new friend was facing. It's likely that Nicholls' discomfort over intrusions into his private life acted as a cautionary tale for Danny – it may even have delayed his decision to join the soap for several years after he was first approached.

Nicholls also wanted to be taken seriously as an actor, and both he and Danny realized the script for *The Trench* – set in the trenches of the First World War – was worth fighting for. Danny had been told he would be up for the part of Victor Dell, a loud-mouthed lad with a gift for the banter and plenty of swagger – obviously, his bread and butter. In the end, Dell cracks under the strain of impending attack and is revealed to be a coward, sobbing as he is forced to climb out of the trench during battle. In the film's DVD extras, Danny says, 'I read the script and I loved it. Just loved the fact that they were so young and vulnerable.' He explained that he was particularly drawn to his character, saying, 'He's the bad one in the bunch, really; it's a good character. He's a bit wild, a bit of a nutter … and he's cockney as well, surprisingly.' Although the role seemed tailor-made for him, Danny had to audition several times before he finally got the part.

The rest of the cast now looks like a who's who of the best of British film and television acting, featuring several faces who would go on to become household names, including Daniel

Craig, Cillian Murphy, Ben Whishaw and James D'Arcy. *The Trench* was an unusual take on the events that took place immediately prior to the infamous Battle of the Somme, the bloodiest and most shocking chapter in the British military's attempts to halt the advancing German army during the First World War. The film is set in one small stretch of a British trench during the forty-eight hours before the troops went 'over the top' to face almost certain death, focusing on a company of mostly teenage volunteers as they go about their daily routine, unaware of what was to come.

Once casting was complete, the boys were gathered, as one group, for rehearsal and a read-through of the script. This is always a tense moment for everyone: the cast and crew's first chance to see if all the individual personalities would fuse. Thankfully, the cast began to gel very quickly, mirroring the friendships and bonds shared by their characters in the film. This camaraderie would be one of the most enjoyable elements in the finished film.

Writer and director William Boyd suggested several books for the actors to read as research, determined the young cast should be well versed in the history of the First World War and fully aware of the hardships endured by the soldiers who fought in it. This included collections of poetry inspired by the events of the war and journals written by the soldiers themselves. Danny recalls in an interview for Sothcott and Mullinger's title, 'It was the first time I had had to do research for a role. [Boyd] gave me these books of poetry by Wilfred Owen. So I was really starting to get a bit more professional, a bit more into it ... I read dozens of books about the First World War and the Battle of the Somme.' Nicholls stated on the film's DVD extras, 'Obviously, you never know, however many books you read, what it felt like in the trench, and to not have slept for three days; so cold that you can't feel your fingers, so hungry that you'd eat anything . . . You can imagine what those things are like if you've got a great imagination, but you can never really get there.'

It would seem Boyd agreed with Nicholls and decided he would have to raise the stakes in order for the actors to feel fully immersed in their roles. Boyd commented, 'We felt it would be really useful to give them just the briefest inkling of what it was like to be in a trench, to sleep out under the stars, to be cold, bored rigid, to be a bit terrified, fed up and hungry.' Thus, the entire cast was told they would be staying out overnight, with everyone assuming it must be a bonding evening in a nearby hotel. Instead, they were shipped off to spend the night sleeping rough in a replica trench in a First World War re-enactment site in Basildon, on the outskirts of London. Boyd justified these extreme measures, reasoning, 'I think that they all knew that it was kind of a test and an opportunity to build up a store of memories and experiences which when they came to the set, or when they came to film or act, they could draw on, because they all had to do sentry duty, they all had to fill sand bags, crawl out in the night on their bellies into the dark Essex countryside. It was real, so when it came to the extraordinary artificiality and oddness of a movie set, they knew what they were being asked to do. It was very valuable.'

Valuable maybe, but this level of 'method' acting was not something Danny was particularly happy about, as he recollected in his autobiography. 'The trench was set up and they started setting off fireworks to try and recreate the terror of the whole thing. To be honest, I started to get the pox with it.' In the movie's DVD special features, Danny explained, 'They just chucked us in this trench at seven o'clock at night until seven o'clock the next day and we had to live like [the characters]. [I] got a feel of it then, sleeping outside, freezing my nuts off – we didn't know what was going on – eating this stew with mud in it, grit in my teeth, and then we had to clean the bowl with bread and [then put] peaches in after. It was heavy. We had nothing to eat all day. It hit me hard.' So hard, in fact, that, following the discovery that one of the other actors had left the trench and returned to London, he and Paul Nicholls jumped ship – in full First World War uniforms and carrying all of their kit! The pair hiked across fields to the nearest train station and headed back to Nicholls' flat in Kilburn. Because neither of them had any cash, they blagged their way onto the train and jumped the barriers at the other end. While this was nothing out of the ordinary for Danny, Nicholls struggled to get through the barrier without being caught and was held by station staff, resulting in both actors having to give their details to the police. With Nicholls as famous as he was at the time, the story made the papers and would serve as one of the first of many brushes Danny would have with the British tabloid press.

Boyd was understandably annoyed at the behaviour of two of his key cast members, but Danny revealed in his book, 'I explained to him that trench life wasn't doing nothing for me and I promised I wouldn't let him down on the job,' telling his director, 'You watch. I'll come through for you.' Danny was true to his word and delivered a strong performance, making the transition from know-it-all to snivelling coward with ease. While the former may not have been much of a stretch, he gives a compelling turn as the latter.

Danny's best scene saw him squaring off with the then unknown Daniel Craig. In an encounter near the end of the film, Danny's character has been caught by Craig's Sergeant

Winter, drunk on the platoon's rum rations and afraid to join his fellow soldiers in the march across no man's land. Winter berates the soldier for his cowardice and uses his boot to push Danny's face into a muddy puddle, trying to drown him. It's a powerful scene and Danny holds his own against the famously intense and physical acting style of the future James Bond.

When *The Trench* was released in UK cinemas in September 1999, it failed to find a large audience. It seemed to fall between two types of market – a bit too arty and theatrical for the mass audience that had turned *Saving Private Ryan* into a blockbuster hit the year before, and not quite literary enough for the art-house crowd. David Rooney in his *Variety* review acknowledged this fact, noting, 'The very confined setting and claustrophobic nature of the material make this a commercially difficult proposal, but careful positioning and critical support may help it find an appreciative audience in select markets.' Rooney praised Boyd's ability to extract strong performances from the predominantly young cast, despite his inexperience as a director.

Danny remembers the film as a hugely positive experience, disclosing in his autobiography that 'It was a tough old job, and it gave me a s**tload of respect for the people who fought in the War.' Danny would also leave the project with newfound admiration for the other actors in the cast, recognizing that the fierce competitiveness he usually felt around his fellow actors could be put to better use – watching and learning, appreciating what could be achieved when a group of actors feed off each other's experience to lift the work to greater heights.

Danny's next job came via a phone call from the film's director rather than through his agent. Renowned Irish playwright and novelist Peter Sheridan had intended to make a film biography about Irish poet and literary legend Brendan Behan. When this long-planned project fell through, Sheridan instead decided to adapt one of Behan's best-known books, *Borstal Boy*, into a film. The autobiographical story had been a successful stage play in the late 1960s and focused on Behan's experiences in a British borstal. At the age of seventeen, Behan had been an active member of the IRA and he was captured on the English mainland during an abortive bombing mission and imprisoned. The story is a coming-of-age tale that sees Behan exploring his budding sexuality, embarking on relationships with an older woman and a male fellow prisoner on a journey of self-examination.

Danny was obviously thrilled to receive a call from such an esteemed figure – Sheridan was part of a well-respected creative family, his brother being Oscar-nominated writer and director Jim Sheridan, whose *In the Name of the Father* had been a huge success a few years earlier – and he was excited about the film as soon as he heard the title. In the movie's DVD commentary, he says, 'I thought *Borstal Boy*, a little hard-nut in a borstal, running about beating everyone up [was] the Daddy! And then I got the script and I'm a gay sailor.' Consequently, Danny had mixed feelings about the whole project. This was the first time a well-known film-maker had contacted him directly, offering him a specific role based purely on what he'd seen Danny do in the past, but the subject matter did bother him. He says in *The Films of Danny Dyer*, 'I was in two minds because I thought the idea that he wants me to play this gay role – at that point in my career it's the last thing you'd think that I'd be known for – [made me feel] really proud because I'd never been seen in that light.' On the other hand, he was worried about what people might make of the subject matter. He joked, 'I just thought, "I'm going to have to act now."'

Danny describes his character, Charlie Milwall, in the commentary: 'He's a young boy, seventeen, who knows who he is sexually and isn't frightened about expressing that he's gay . . . to be in a borstal and to be openly gay, it's gotta be a nightmare. That's what makes him such a strong character – he's like, "I'm gay and that's that."'

It was with this same determination and courage that Danny approached the part. He was clear he wanted to avoid playing Charlie as effeminate, unwilling to pander to the assumption that a character's sexual orientation would have any bearing on his outward appearance or mannerisms. The audience's acceptance of Charlie and all his relationships in the film – with the other prisoners as well as with Brendan – hinged on him creating a young man who was both likeable and relatable as well as open and confident about being gay. In the hands of another actor, the character could have become clichéd and easily unbalanced the whole film.

Danny's main co-star, playing the lead role of Brendan, was young American actor Shawn Hatosy. It may seem an unusual choice, an American being chosen to portray such a beloved and respected Irish figure, but Hatosy had started making a name for himself in supporting roles in some very successful Hollywood films, including *The Faculty*, *Double Jeopardy*, *In and Out*, as well as a high-profile turn opposite Kevin Costner in 1997's mega-flop, *The Postman*, demonstrating he had earned the right to tackle a more challenging part. Hatosy has since forged a long and respected career on US television, most notably as Detective Sammy Bryant in the controversial and groundbreaking LA-based cop show, *Southland*.

Regardless of Hatosy's big-screen accomplishments, Danny didn't really take to his co-star. But, rather than allow this to be a problem, Danny decided to use the tension and underlying distrust in his performance, making it easier to maintain the anger burning in Charlie during the early stage of their relationship, when the latter's affection went unrequited. The scene Danny was most anxious about was the moment the two boys finally kiss. In his autobiography, Danny stated, 'You can call on all your resources, but I don't care who you are, if it doesn't float your boat, you're not going to be able to enjoy the moment.' Yet this was also one of the main reasons he'd taken the part in the first place – to test himself as an actor and push the boundaries of what people expected of him. He said, prior to filming the scene, 'A full-on passionate kiss is going to be heavy . . . I know I'm going to do the job well, there's no other way. Once I've done that, I know I can do anything, there's nothing in this game that can hold me back.' He then added with a typically cheeky grin, 'I've just got to put my tongue in his mouth.'

In all, it was an extraordinary education for Danny and he rose to the challenge admirably. He had been very nervous about what his father would make of his character and the gay elements of the story, but in the end Danny could tell his performance had won him over; he was proud of his determination to make his character as real as possible.

Borstal Boy was a modest success, understandably being more of a hit in Ireland and eventually becoming a cult-classic in the gay community upon its DVD release. The film did not appear on DVD for a couple of years after its cinematic release, however, and was eventually picked up by a distribution company who, by releasing works Danny had been attached to previously, were trying to cash in on his later success. The film sold well in excess of 300,000 copies – but mostly to a public who were expecting a completely different film. The DVD cover only had Danny's name above the title, with no mention of Shawn Hatosy, and the artwork featured an image of a considerably older Danny, playing on his hard-man image and the film's misleading and provocative title. This was the first and by no means the last time Danny's name and image would be used to trick his fan base in order to sell a film, and it was an issue that would cause him, and his career, serious problems in the future.

Danny's determination to keep pushing himself was about to pay off. He had played three very different characters in his first three films – a drug-taking clubber, a cowardly First World War soldier and an openly gay borstal inmate. His resolve to rise to any challenge had not gone unnoticed and he would soon be given the opportunity to make some brave and unexpected choices about his future as an actor.

CHAPTER FIVE

STAGE ONE

At the beginning of 2000, Danny was at an important crossroads in his career. He had been pursued by another agency, ICM, and had made the decision to leave Charlotte Kelly and join the much larger firm. If it was a difficult choice personally, professionally it made sense. ICM was one of the biggest talent agencies in the world, looking after numerous actors, directors and authors, and would hopefully open a multitude of new doors for him.

Yet despite the extra muscle behind him, Danny's career had entered a strange period of limbo, as a succession of supporting roles had started coming his way without him having to fight too hard to get them. He was losing focus and, in turn, the drive that had fuelled his love of acting since his early teens was fading. It was all too easy and the lack of a challenge, coupled with his continuing use of drink and drugs, was making him lazy and jaded. That all-important leading role still eluded him and the impact Danny had made with his first three films – and the professional clout that went with it – was rapidly beginning to diminish. Salvation came from the most unlikely place – his old friend Paul Nicholls, whom Danny had remained friends with after their time together on *The Trench*.

Nicholls called Danny in a fluster of excitement, having

been summoned to an audition for a part in a new play by Harold Pinter entitled *Celebration*. Danny had received notice to attend the same audition, but not knowing who Pinter was, had been slightly less enthusiastic about it, stating in his book, 'I told [Nicholls] I'd never heard of the geezer, and I was telling the truth.' Danny's agent was ecstatic, advising him this was a once-in-a lifetime experience. He recalled, 'She said, "He hasn't written a play in fifteen years. This is a new play. This is a massive opportunity for you. I really need you to learn the dialogue." I was like, "Whatever, I'll go and do it."' Danny would later tell Jonathan Ross, in an interview on his ITV chat show, what a momentous, life-changing experience their first meeting was. 'I loved the play. I loved the work and I got it and I walked in, straight up to him [Pinter] and I said, "How you doin', son?" And the whole room was going, "F****n' hell", and he liked that. I think he respected that and we became really close.'

Of course, Danny was no stranger to the stage. Just after *Prime Suspect*, in between filming numerous supporting roles on television, he had appeared in the play *Not Gods But Giants* and later, during the extended period of unemployment while waiting for *Human Traffic* to be released in 1999, he took a role in a celebrated production of *Certain Young Men*, written and directed by Peter Gill.

A respected figure in British theatre, Gill had built a reputation as a unique and gifted storyteller. Danny turned up to the audition without having read a script – in fact, he had no choice, as not one word of the play had been written. Gill famously writes only after the actors have been cast, building the play during the run-up to rehearsals and incorporating elements of the actors' personalities. This free-form approach did not particularly suit Danny. He was uncomfortable at the audition, preferring to let his acting do the talking, but Gill saw something different in him, and cast him on the spot.

So began a period of what Danny describes in *Straight Up* as 'two weeks of yak'. The other seven actors were much more comfortable with the process, being more experienced and hailing from the traditional drama school background, leaving Danny feeling somewhat isolated. But he was quick to realize all the sitting around and talking was worth it as soon as he was handed the finished script. Crafted over the weeks of Gill's observation, it was more than Danny could have hoped for. The story revolved around the lives of eight gay men, examining their relationships and dissecting what being in a gay couple means to each of the men as individuals. Danny's character was written as a predatory gay man who uses seduction and sex to get what he wants from those around him. He told *Attitude*, the UK's leading gay magazine, 'That interests me more than being camp and clichéd.'

Confident he could inhabit the character Gill had built around him, Danny regained faith in his own abilities, and as he took to the rehearsal stage the other actors started to sit up and take notice. Again, Danny fed off his own highly competitive nature to suppress the long-held feelings of insecurity he tended to suffer around more experienced actors. The contempt he often held towards fellow cast members was not necessarily him looking to better them, it was more a tool used to gain recognition as an equal. In his autobiography he says, 'Respect from your peers is what you crave as an actor … You get a fan base, you get people in the street recognizing you, but what you really want is people in the same game as you to look at you and say, "He's good."'

The play had middling success, with most critics

acknowledging the performances but failing to understand Gill's intended purpose in exploring this particular set of characters or their lives.

Danny came away from the production having experienced a method of working that would remain unique for the rest of his career. It gave him more belief in his skills, and won him an unexpected, but expanding, gay fan base. This legion of new admirers would remain quietly loyal to Danny for many years to come, becoming increasingly more important in later years.

Now, though, Danny needed to convince Harold Pinter, one of Britain's greatest playwrights, that he was worthy of joining his new play.

Like Danny, Harold Pinter was born and raised in East London; however, that's where the similarities end. Pinter was middle class and had been well educated at the Royal Academy of Dramatic Arts. Starting out as an actor, he soon developed a flair for writing and directing and was eventually recognized as a truly exceptional talent within the British theatrical community. His long and distinguished career saw his work receive countless awards while his style, eloquently described by critic Irvine Wardle as the 'comedy of menace', would even coin its own descriptive term, 'Pinteresque' becoming shorthand for, as the *Oxford English Dictionary* puts it, 'implications of threat and strong feeling produced through colloquial language, apparent triviality, and long pauses'. Unlike Peter Gill, Pinter's work is so tightly scripted, each word (and pause) is precisely placed so as to convey a specific meaning and to create maximum impact. There is comparatively little interpretation needed by the actor, with the words, literally, doing all the talking.

As soon as Danny read the script for *Celebration*, he knew

it was on a different level to everything he'd read for before. It played to his strengths and, he was sure, would allow him to shine. He revealed in *Straight Up*, '*Celebration* was a fair cut above some of the other stuff I've done. It was a great monologue, really musical in the way the words are used. I loved it and that made it easy to learn.'

Danny's increasing confidence as a stage actor came from his fundamental need to keep pushing himself and there was no denying he thrived on the adrenaline rush closely associated with live performance. This desire to keep growing professionally went hand in hand with an understanding of the distinct lack of financial reward involved in this line of work. But, at this stage of his career at least, money was rarely a deciding factor in his decision-making process. Thus, despite not knowing who he was, Danny realized a chance to work with and learn from Harold Pinter meant more than the accompanying salary, and he was determined to win the respect of the great man himself.

Being put up against his friend Paul Nicholls was the only negative aspect of going for *Celebration*. But it would seem that ignorance is indeed bliss as Danny's no-nonsense approach to the audition process and lack of awareness regarding Pinter seemed to make everything go his way. According to his autobiography, when Danny was introduced to Pinter, he simply walked up to him and asked if he could get up and show what he could do. What may seem like irreverence and disrespect to some was seen as refreshingly blunt by Pinter, who warmed to the actor immediately. Danny recalls, 'I got right on that stage, and I smashed it first time. It really did flow for me. I was at total ease with it … I always know a good writer, because the words roll off the tongue like you wouldn't believe.'

Danny heard he'd got the job by the end of the day, and thus began a long and unlikely working relationship and friendship that would last for almost a decade, only ending with Pinter's death in 2008. As with most theatre work, and alluded to above, the job was not particularly well paid – a weekly salary that would seem like a pittance even against the most meagre of independent film salaries. The hours are long – often stretching to eight performances a week – but the professional kudos is invaluable. Danny would love it.

The actors met at the Almeida Theatre's rehearsal rooms in Islington, North London and Danny was introduced to the rest of the cast – Lindsay Duncan, Lia Williams and Keith Allen – and despite not feeling particularly nervous himself, after a short period of time he began to notice the other actors' worry about working with Pinter. Famous for his attention to detail and ability to erupt in anger at his actors during rehearsal, Danny noted in his book, 'You pick up on everyone else's attitude to him. That said, the atmosphere was intense but it wasn't nasty.'

As with the audition, Danny took to the writing and never seemed to get on the wrong side of the great man. Indeed, they struck up an easy friendship, bonding over a mutual love of football, and West Ham in particular. Danny felt an instant connection with Pinter, respecting and responding to the man rather than his reputation, and he assumed the feeling was mutual: 'I think he saw how raw I was and how much I wanted to learn.' He concluded, 'I think he liked me, too.'

Danny formed an equally strong, if somewhat different, relationship with his fellow cast member, Keith Allen. Allen had a well-deserved reputation as a bit of a hell-raiser and proved to be a significant influence on an already slightly out-of-control Danny. The pair would spend their evenings 'tearing it up' in London's Soho, tumbling into rehearsals, slightly worse for wear, the next day. Both received stern warnings from Pinter and, temporarily at least, got their heads down and concentrated on the work at hand. After a long rehearsal period, the play opened at the Almeida Theatre on 16 March 2000. Celebration ran as part of a double bill with another of Pinter's older plays, *The Room*, with much of the cast, excluding Danny, appearing in both.

The reviews were almost unanimous in their praise, and Danny was able to bask in the shared glory of a successful production. It's fair to say that any cast involved in a Pinter play is often overlooked for individual plaudits, as many consider that with such high-quality writing there is little room for interpretation, but Danny knew he had done a great job and felt Pinter was particularly pleased with what he had achieved. Danny recalled in an interview with the *Independent*, 'He would trust you as an actor. That was the reason he hired you, because he didn't want some stress actor who needed a pat on the arse every two minutes . . . I just felt more intelligent being around him. He was a real inspiration for me.'

It had been a life-changing episode for Danny. He had pushed himself way out of his comfort zone and had surprised many, including himself, with how well he'd managed to make the transition from screen to 'respectable' stage actor. The experience had given him renewed confidence in his ability and strengthened his resolve to persevere in his chosen profession. He still had one major ambition left to achieve: he had his sights firmly set on landing the lead role in a major film.

While that particular goal was certainly attainable, it was, frustratingly, still a few rungs further up the career ladder for Danny. Luckily, he was about to make the acquaintance of one man who would give him a very important leg-up and become a guiding light during the next stage of Danny's career. He was about to meet Nick Love.

CHAPTER SIX

ALL YOU NEED IS LOVE

Although things were starting to look up professionally for Danny, privately he was not in a great place. His drinking and drug use were getting worse, but still he did not view it as a problem. He continued to land some solid roles and on set he was turning in strong performances, yet it seemed that a reliable stream of work had given him a false sense of security.

While he might have been making enough of a name for himself to ensure a steady number of offers came his way, Danny's early determination to keep progressing his career was no longer being reflected in the jobs he chose to pursue and accept. It appeared that the recognition he was receiving from inside the industry, as well as the first trappings of fame and success, were beginning to turn his head, making him considerably more complacent.

Danny has never really had a problem with keeping his feet on the ground, but during this period he neglected to think about what was best for Joanne or Dani, let alone himself. Luckily, he had people around him who kept his best interests at heart. Paul Nicholls was one such person, and would check in with Danny every now and again to make sure he was still (mostly) on the straight and narrow.

Nicholls' own career was going from strength to strength.

It's easy to imagine that his post-*EastEnders* pin-up status ensured he was first on the list for the most sought-after projects, and the shrewd young actor had amassed an impressive network of contacts within the industry. He was constantly meeting the latest up-and-coming writers and directors – most of whom realized a project with Nicholls' name attached had a much better chance of getting made. Nick Love was one of these talented figures.

Love had a similar background to Danny. Growing up in 1970s London, his drug use at an early age had seen him spend a spell in rehab. However, he learned from his mistakes, turned his life around and managed to get a place in film school. He worked hard to establish himself in the right circles and was emerging as a strong working-class voice in what was at the time an almost exclusively middle-class British film industry. Love was an energetic and engaging presence, someone who had no problem selling himself, with an unwavering confidence in his own abilities as a film-maker. It was no surprise, then, that he thrived in the endless cut and thrust of the industry, finding it a natural home for his talents. And when Danny finally met him, he was ready to direct his first feature movie.

Love had made waves the previous year with a short picture entitled *Love Story*. The film delivered enough of an idea of what Love could achieve, and it wasn't long before he and co-writer Dominic Eames had written a script for the piece that would become his directorial debut, *Goodbye Charlie Bright*.

Nicholls was already attached to the project, having signed on to play the film's title character, when he suggested Danny come along and meet the director. Nicholls insisted they would get on, saying Love reminded him of Danny.

His instinct proved correct. From the moment the pair shook hands, there was instant chemistry; they were soon swapping stories and revelling in each other's enthusiasm for film-making and acting.

Love talked passionately about his forthcoming project, telling Danny he would make sure there was a role in it for him, and, true to his word, an offer came through within days. Danny was excited to get the chance to work with Love, but he was disappointed he wouldn't be playing the main protagonist in the film. He was convinced he could play the part better: he understood where Charlie came from, having been brought up on a housing estate with a gang of mates – he had already lived the role through his childhood and teens. Love was willing to hear Danny's argument, and he may even have agreed he was a better fit, but Nicholls was a considerably bigger name than Danny at the time, and his involvement with the project was key to getting it into production. So, having aired his view, he nonetheless excitedly accepted the smaller, but pivotal, role of Francis.

Goodbye Charlie Bright was set on a housing estate and was filmed on location in South London. The action centres on a gang of young men who have grown up together and spend most of their time hanging around the tower blocks drinking, indulging in casual sex and the odd bit of petty crime. Nicholls' character, Charlie, is the obvious leader of the gang and his best friend is Justin (played by Roland Manookian). The story reveals how Charlie and Justin ultimately have different expectations of their life, causing the gang to drift apart and Charlie and Justin's relationship to suffer irreparable damage.

Danny's character, however, has already distanced himself from the boys, instead choosing to spend more time with a girl from the estate. While Danny's character appears passive and a bit soft in his early scenes, it's clear he could relate to Francis – his relationship with Joanne and the birth of his daughter Dani when he was still a teenager had had a dramatic and sobering effect on his life. Danny brings an air of crushed desperation to the role when Francis' girlfriend is revealed to have been cheating on him; he is pushed to his limits as he sees his whole future evaporating before his eyes, and it is this vulnerability that establishes such a strong connection with the audience. The juxtaposition of defeated powerlessness and defiance makes it so much more emotive than just another violent retaliation scene.

Danny's performance delivered more than Love could have hoped for from a relatively small role. The pair's bond and mutual admiration was strengthened by the fact that Paul Nicholls had suffered a crisis of confidence on the shoot, which they had had to deal with together. Perhaps he was all too aware that Danny was more or less perfect for the part he himself was playing and worried he might be replaced. Whatever the reason, his insecurity had been a major headache for Love, on what was his first major project as a director.

For Danny, his most valuable experience from his time on *Goodbye Charlie Bright* was in gaining a sense of what it was like to work with a real film-maker – an artist, rather than a 'jobbing' director. While the pair may have had many things in common, helping forge an unusually strong personal and professional relationship, late night partying wasn't one of them – Love had completely cleaned up his act after his spell in rehab and rarely even touched a drink. But, at last, there was someone Danny could really relate to in his chosen profession: a fellow working-class Londoner, passionate and driven, and established enough to help his career along. It looked like he had found the perfect role model.

The film was released in May 2001 but failed to make much of an impact in UK cinemas. While never likely to have quite the same impact as *Trainspotting* or *Human Traffic*, the film stands up today as a similarly evocative snapshot of a time and place in British youth culture, with its cool soundtrack featuring rising UK stars such as Craig David, Artful Dodger and Mis-Teeq, and a Britpop anthem from Oasis over the film's climactic scenes that also captured the sound of the era.

Almost immediately after he had wrapped on *Goodbye Charlie Bright*, Danny landed another part in a TV film being made by Sky, *Is Harry on the Boat?*. Although it was to be his first real lead role, the main draw for Danny was the chance to shoot the film on location – in Ibiza.

The moment Danny stepped off the plane, he noticed something strange: wherever he went on the island, virtually everyone seemed to know who he was. Most would offer to buy him a drink, while many simply gave him a pill and invited him to hang out with them. The combination of being many miles from home, the ego massage he was receiving from this constant recognition and the 'anything goes' atmosphere on the island was about to create a perfect storm of debauchery and careless behaviour. It would send Danny's life into a dramatic tailspin, one that would cost him personally and see him become increasingly reliant on a heady mix of drink and drugs.

Ibiza had grown into the ultimate party destination, playing host to some of the biggest and most popular dance clubs in the world. These 'super-clubs' had become the new spiritual home of the club culture *Human Traffic* brought so vividly to life. At almost exactly the same time Danny set foot on the island, the film's cult status was reaching critical mass and anyone even vaguely connected to it was soon enjoying near legendary status. The fact that Danny had played Moff, the pilled-up party animal everybody wanted to take drugs with, meant he was welcomed with open arms everywhere he went. The only problem was that the punters thought they were on a night out with Moff, and Danny, not wanting to disappoint them, was more than willing to play along.

Over the course of the shoot Danny rarely had to put his hand in his pocket. The 24/7 party lifestyle, which might be sustainable for a two-week holiday, started to take its toll on him as work on the film continued. He was in virtually every scene, but was too spaced-out to fully appreciate his star billing. For the first time since he had committed to acting as a career, what had always been easy was now a struggle. He would turn up to set late, start drinking and then couldn't remember his lines. His complacency was magnified by the drugs, and he started to get on the wrong side of the producers. They told him to pull himself together, but Danny knew it would be virtually impossible to fire him and still finish the project on time and within budget. Danny was out of control and it was now having an effect on his health; towards the end of the shoot he was so run down that he had an ulcer in one eye and the crew were forced to film all his scenes from one angle.

Around September 2000, Ibiza was entering its end-of-season climax and Danny and the rest of the cast were more than happy to be carried along for the ride. Danny was inebriated most of the time and got involved with one of the actresses from the movie, Davinia Taylor. Taylor's father, Alan Murphy, had made a fortune in business, which provided his daughter with independent wealth. She had dropped out of acting courses when she was younger and had since become a core member of London's Primrose Hill set, mixing with the likes of Jude Law, Sadie Frost, Kate Moss and Jonny Lee Miller, and eventually stumbled back into acting via modelling. She took a role in *Hollyoaks*, but it was not clear if she wanted to pursue acting full-time. There was no doubting Davinia was a beautiful girl, but she had nothing in common with Danny, their backgrounds being so different. It's not difficult to imagine what was going on – Danny was 'off the leash' and, if he was thinking at all, probably assumed he was far enough away from home to get away with an affair without anyone ever finding out. What he hadn't considered was the fact that in this world – the world of non-stop clubbing and drugs – he might as well be the most famous person on the planet. He was Moff from *Human Traffic*. That made him a big fish in a small pond and that in turn made him a target for the paparazzi. This would be Danny's first real brush with the tabloid press and it was going to cost him dearly.

Back in the UK, the first Joanne knew about Danny's dalliance was from seeing pictures of him with Taylor splashed across the celebrity gossip pages of the *Sun*. She was understandably devastated. If things had been bad between her and Danny before he left for Ibiza, she had assumed it was just another phase and that they'd manage to work out their problems as they always had – together. By his own admission, Danny had not been paying enough attention to Joanne and Dani for a while, as he confirmed in his autobiography: 'I was cracking on doing my thing, which was mostly looking after Dani and occasionally getting b*llocked by Joanne for trying to live the life of Jack the Lad and leaving her to care for the kid.' He confessed, 'I was also out on one quite a lot, which was unfair to the family.'

In early 2001, when *Is Harry on the Boat?* was finally finished, Danny flew home to London, but, with his private life as it was, he didn't even try to patch things up with Joanne – he knew it was a lost cause. Instead of going home, he moved straight into Taylor's London home. At that point Taylor was living in the mansion known as Supernova Heights in London's Primrose Hill, which she had famously bought from Oasis star Noel Gallagher in late December 1999. Local residents had celebrated after hearing news of Gallagher selling up, tired of the late-night comings and goings and loud parties. But it wasn't long before Supernova Heights was hitting the headlines again as a safe haven and non-stop party palace for many of London's bright young things.

It is a testament to Danny's drive to keep his career going during a period in which his personal life was so unbalanced and his dependence on drink and drugs was becoming unmanageable that he was still working. He was finally being offered roles without having to audition, but, in what was to become a dangerous habit for him, he began accepting roles not because they were interesting or even well paid, but because they were being handed to him on a plate.

This trait of taking what was immediately on offer started a little earlier in his career. This can be seen in his acceptance of a supporting role in *Greenfingers*, a British comedy set in an open prison, which aimed to do for prisoners and flower arranging what *The Full Monty* had done for unemployed steel workers and stripping. Unfortunately, the film failed to connect with an audience and disappeared without trace at the UK box office. In the end, the only notable thing about the film was the fact it reunited Danny with Helen Mirren, his *Prime Suspect* co-star, after almost a decade.

With his desire to really stretch himself seemingly dwindling, Danny started to accept more roles that could be perceived as a step backwards in terms of him reaching his goal of becoming a lead film actor. In 2001, he gave another comedic performance in *High Heels and Low Lifes*, a British comedy-drama directed by Mel Smith.

Smith had risen to fame with *Not the Nine O'Clock News* before his comedy double-act with Griff Rhys Jones spawned a hit BBC comedy sketch show that ran for several series. He had huge success as a director with the transfer of Rowan Atkinson's Mr Bean character from television to the big screen – 1997's *Bean* made more than £150 million around the world from an estimated £11 million budget, and still stands as one of the most profitable British films ever made.

Many believed that *High Heels* would have the same international appeal as *The Full Monty* and *Four Weddings and a Funeral*, and the budget was set accordingly – at almost £8 million, it was considerably more than the average British film. This was Danny's biggest budget project to date. He had his own trailer and began to feel he was leading a charmed life. The movie would see Danny play his first role as a gangster – albeit a humorous version of one – and the largely slapstick tone meant he knew he wouldn't have to stretch himself too much. The final cut ended up a little too light-hearted, however, and struggled to break even on its cinematic release, relying on DVD sales and foreign markets to pull it out of the red after disappointing UK and US box office takes.

While the work itself left him cold, Danny was thrilled to meet Mel Smith, a man who famously enjoyed sharing his love for the finer things in life with those around him. He held extravagant dinner parties and entertained many of the most fascinating and talented people working in film and television at the time. Danny relished the opportunity to experience a lifestyle that had for so long been off-limits to someone with his background. He felt he was finally being accepted by his peers, and being judged on his acting ability rather than on who he was or where he'd come from. He began to get carried away with his acting abilities, feeling indestructible, untouchable, as he reveals in *The Films of Danny Dyer*: 'I'm passionate about [acting] and it comes easy and naturally to me and they're paying me for it . . . I'm meeting amazing people . . . I'm getting out of the f*****g homophobic, racist, East London mentality, I'm feeling a bit cultured . . . I'm going to dinner parties and I'm meeting amazing people and I just feel like I'm really f*****g spreading my wings a bit.' He concluded, '[Those were] really good times in my life then. It seemed like I was just doing quality stuff as well . . . and I just thought, "Wow, this is never going to end."'

While it was far from the end, Danny was still on a steep downward slope in terms of his drinking and drug-taking and it began to affect his reputation in the industry. While the offers were still coming in, and many did not require any form of audition, the types of roles on offer were all beginning to look worryingly similar.

Around this period, he was also approached about a role in *Mean Machine*, a remake of Burt Reynolds' 1974 comedy *The Longest Yard*, which was being built around former footballer turned actor Vinnie Jones. The original movie had seen a group of prisoners challenge their guards to a game of American football; the British adaptation would, of course, switch the American sport for soccer.

Jones had broken into acting through his iconic, but virtually silent, appearance in Guy Ritchie's *Lock, Stock and Two Smoking Barrels* in 1998, before teaming back up with the director for *Snatch*. He also won supporting roles in a couple of big Hollywood movies: *Gone in 60 Seconds* with Nicholas Cage and Angelina Jolie, and *Swordfish* with John Travolta, Hugh Jackman and Halle Berry. This would be Jones' first starring role and many, including Danny, had doubts Jones was really leading man material. In *The Films of Danny Dyer* he says, 'It was a big ask for Vinnie Jones to be able to step into Burt Reynolds' shoes . . . I just didn't really rate [Vinnie] as an actor.'

Danny didn't have a particularly good time on the film. After a couple of very positive early meetings with the writers and director, things went rapidly downhill as soon as they arrived on set for filming. Nothing could detract from the fact it was a fairly small part for Danny at this stage in his career. It didn't help that he felt isolated from what he describes in Sothcott and Mullinger's book as 'all the Lock, Stock mob', who formed a fairly impenetrable clique. He recalls, 'It was a strange experience. It wasn't really one that I enjoyed much . . . they didn't really know me – they knew of me, but they'd be playing cards at lunchtime and stuff, and I wasn't really invited into their little circle.'

He did make one contact on the production, however: the producer Matthew Vaughn, who was a big fan of Danny's work. Danny recalls, 'He gave me the book to *Layer Cake*, because obviously he was thinking of me playing the lead role.' Unfortunately, a few misjudged comments about Vaughn's friend and producing partner Guy Ritchie at the *Mean Machine* premiere soured their relationship and it would be Daniel Craig who would eventually take the lead in the movie version of Vaughn's *Layer Cake*. (This was the part many believe first convinced producers of the Bond franchise that Craig had something special, and could have acted as his unofficial audition for the role of 007 in *Casino Royale*.) It wasn't the first time and it certainly wouldn't be the last time that Danny's comments in interviews would lose him work or cause him trouble with the press.

Like a big dark cloud, a general feeling of dissatisfaction was settling over Danny. In some respects, things looked like they were going well – he was always working – but, in truth, his career was in limbo. Far from being offered the prime roles he knew could progress his career to the next level – roles he was confident he was more than capable of playing – he was drowning in a sea of supporting parts. Danny was ready to carry a film, and as he watched other people playing characters he'd gone for and failed to land, or worse still, ones he knew he could handle but had never been offered, his ego started getting in the way. He wasn't afraid to express his dissatisfaction with the roles he was being offered and soon that displeasure turned to bitterness. It affected his reputation and latterly, the amount of work he was offered.

At the same time, he was in denial about his personal life. Despite living in a huge mansion with a beautiful new girlfriend, Danny was missing his family. Joanne and Dani were only a small part of his new, glamorous world, and he struggled with that loss. Yet again he found himself trying to numb the pain with pills and alcohol, while desperately looking for something to spark his imagination and rekindle his passion for acting. Both would get worse before they got better, but it is surprising that the first step in Danny's eventual recovery, both personally and professionally, saw him return to stage acting, and involved him surrendering his fate, yet again, to one of British theatre's most respected writers and directors. Danny was about to renew his acquaintance with Harold Pinter.

CHAPTER SEVEN

STAGE TWO

Danny, and many others, had seen his collaboration with Harold Pinter on *Celebration* as a professional turning point, believing it would lead to him tackling weightier material and greater challenges. He'd been pleased with what he'd achieved during the play's London run and had come away from the project with renewed excitement about the myriad possibilities a career in acting could offer. His reinvigorated focus and drive also set him up nicely for his meeting with Nick Love.

So, when the original cast of *Celebration* was given the opportunity to reunite and take the production to New York in 2001, they all jumped at it. The play would run for a handful of performances as part of a wider celebration of Pinter's work, to be staged at the Lincoln Center in the heart of Manhattan. Under the guidance of Pinter, Danny felt certain he would get some of his old focus back, as there was no denying that the year between the play opening in London and its transfer to New York had seen his personal situation dramatically worsen.

However, it appeared that the New York run would provide nothing of the sort. Since hooking up with Taylor, Danny had been enjoying the trappings of his new celebrity status and it wasn't long before he started getting into more trouble. It is easy to speculate that this non-stop party lifestyle interfered with his work, but Danny's career was by now virtually on hold: he refused any big jobs for months at a time, meaning he more or less disappeared from the big screen for the next three years. His ego had got the better of him and he preferred to live as a famous actor rather than work as a moderately successful one, stifling any professional progress he might have been making. With Taylor on his arm, his day-to-day business was starting to fill gossip columns and his night-time antics attracted the kind of press attention reserved for the likes of the Beckhams.

Danny recalled this period in his autobiography: 'Things went nuts for me. I was desperately unhappy to be parted from Joanne and Dani. In fact, I've never been lower in my life.' He added, 'I think that's the worst thing on earth, being separated from your kid. Anything I've been through, all the b*llocks the press has thrown at me over the years . . . nothing comes close to losing your kid from your life. I'd take all the crap that has come my way a million times over rather than go through that again.'

In early 2001, his relationship with Davinia Taylor seemed to be moving at breakneck speed, and the *Mirror* reported that Danny had proposed to Taylor while on safari in Kenya, claiming, 'They haven't set a date – but who knows if they will make it to the altar given [Davinia's] record.'

But as time passed, Danny was growing more and more uncomfortable with the celebrity couple status he now shared with Taylor, and longed to reconnect with his old life as a partner to Joanne and a loving father to Dani. Consequently, the call from Pinter could not have come at a better time. It gave Danny time to pause, draw breath and think about what was important to him.

Danny had embraced Pinter's mentorship and the friendship that blossomed between the pair. He spent time at

Pinter's home, socializing with the playwright and his wife, Lady Antonia Fraser, on numerous occasions. Their approval had made him feel worthy of the praise he was receiving as an actor and in turn, he gave some of the best performances of his career during *Celebration*'s London run.

By the time of the New York transfer, things were very different. Drugs had become an everyday part of Danny's life, and he was drinking more than ever. So, while he could take stock and appreciate what he was missing – namely, his family – the emotional pain it caused also compounded and continued his problems. (We have already seen how the death of his grandfather led him to turn to drugs as a method of coping.)

When the play opened in New York in July 2001, Danny had almost hit rock bottom, and his personal issues were about to cross over into his professional life. It came to a head on 24 July, the night of his twenty-fourth birthday. Danny had brought Taylor with him and the pair embraced the party scene in the Big Apple with the same ravenous enthusiasm that they did in London. Unfortunately for Danny, this meant an unhealthy escalation in the type of drugs he was using. He had rapidly progressed from cannabis and ecstasy to cocaine, but knew he was taking it to another level as he was introduced to crack. He was going out every night with a group of wealthy socialites in the trendy Meatpacking District of the city before sneaking back to the cast's hotel and taking 'downers' to enable him to get some sleep prior to the next day's performance. He admitted to Jonathan Ross on his chat show, 'I got too excited. I over-indulge. I thought I could over-indulge and walk out on stage and do a play. Of course, it's just ridiculous.'

On this particular occasion he was in an exceptionally bad way, arriving at the theatre just in time for his entrance, struggling on stage for his (mercifully silent) first scene. By the time his main speech came, Danny could barely think straight. He explained to Ross, 'I was bang in trouble. I went on the stage. I didn't have a clue what to say . . . I'm meant to interject into a conversation . . . all the actors looked round and I haven't got a clue what to say. I could see the fear in their eyes.' During his big scene, playing a waiter who interrupts the main characters as they eat, Danny opened his mouth to say his lines . . . and nothing came out. His mind had gone blank, and not just for the lines of the play, but even for any form of improvisation. A Pinter play might be famous for its long pauses, but the audience expects there to be some dialogue either side of those pauses. Pinter's plays run like clockwork, and without Danny's lines the whole thing ground to a halt. He describes the feeling in his book, stating, 'The worst thing about it was that I was looking down at the other actors and they all started to shrink into their seats and look at me as if to say, "Oh my God. Please don't do this to us." I was putting them right in the s**t.' After a prompt from one of the other actors, Danny was jolted back on track and delivered his lines before leaving the stage. He stood sobbing in the wings – the relief, embarrassment and disappointment washing over him. The rest of the cast were quick to offer consolations, reassuring him it happens to the best of actors and not to let it affect him too much. It's doubtful they would have been quite as sympathetic if they'd known the whole story.

Keith Allen was far less forgiving. He was fully aware of Danny's problems with drugs and booze, and took him aside and told him to pull himself together. Danny told Jonathan Ross, 'You never forget that moment. I needed something to happen and all of a sudden I thought, "Well sort your life out – lively." I had a great opportunity, I was a very lucky actor to be working with such people and I nearly blew it – just 'cos I wanted to get off my nut, basically.' He concluded, 'It takes a serious moment like that for you to go, "Right, rein it in . . . It will never happen to me again."'

It turned out to be just the wake-up call Danny needed, and he cleaned up his act – temporarily, at least – and finished the New York run without further incident. But the whole experience had been tainted for him, and any excitement he had been feeling about his return to stage acting had quickly evaporated. He went home to England feeling he had lost something vital in his performance: his natural fearlessness had vanished and he decided he didn't want to do any more theatre. Afraid he would suffer another mental block, he was unwilling to challenge his insecurities or ever again put himself in a position that would make him feel so vulnerable and exposed.

It was surprising, then, that within a year he would accept another direct invitation from Pinter, this time to join the cast of *No Man's Land* for an extended run at the National Theatre in London, with a countrywide tour to follow. Danny thought long and hard, but knew it was too good an opportunity to turn down, having appreciated that 'getting straight back on the horse' was probably the best approach to conquering the stage fright that had crippled him in New York. The deciding factor may also have been the realization that a six-month run in a high-profile production, working with his mentor Harold Pinter, might just be the stabilizing influence he needed at this time and could help him forget the private sadness he felt at being separated from Joanne and Dani.

Danny admits that he never really got to grips with the play in terms of understanding its subtle meanings and themes – even after a long rehearsal period, six months on stage and a handful of touring performances – but it definitely cured any mental block he'd been suffering. The whole experience was a blur, mostly due to the fact that, despite his best intentions, he was still partying virtually every night after the show. He had managed to steer clear of crack cocaine, but drugs were nevertheless a much-needed crutch.

Danny's professional unhappiness was deepened by a phone call he received from Pinter himself during the rehearsal period for the play. He told Danny he had been diagnosed with cancer and feared he was too ill to continue directing, handing over control to an assistant. This was a bitter blow to Danny, not only in terms of what it meant for the immediate future of the production, but on a much more personal level, as he recalled the slow, painful death of his granddad. He said in *Straight Up*, 'It was a horrendous feeling when I thought about the struggle he had in front of him. I really liked Harold, I worshipped him, really. I loved how he didn't conform to anything. I loved the fact that all these poncey critics were frightened of him … When he was part of the company, I felt strong; without him I felt weak.'

Danny felt isolated from the National Theatre crowd, and had little in common with any of the other actors in the cast. To compensate, he became trapped in the same destructive cycle as in New York: leaving the theatre, partying all night, taking pills to get some sleep and waking just in time to return to work for curtain-up. He didn't make any more catastrophic errors on stage, but during the first leg of the London run, on New Year's Day, he got himself into hot water by giving his understudy advance warning that he was intending to feign illness and not show up for work. Danny in fact thought he was doing a good deed by giving his understudy a chance to take centre stage for one performance, but it just served as an illustration of his lack of understanding of theatre tradition, and further highlighted the fact he would always struggle to be fully accepted into their world. The rest of the cast were furious and ignored Danny off stage for practically the remainder of the run.

This wouldn't have been so bad if it wasn't for the fact he still had several national tour dates ahead of him. Playing to the National Theatre audiences was one thing, but the show did not have the same appeal when it started to tour the more provincial venues, and they found themselves playing to half-empty theatres across the country. Danny was getting more depressed, spending nights out alone and drinking heavily. This had its own unfortunate irony in the fact that, while he felt so low, Pinter had actually placed him in a much sought-after position. He relates in his autobiography how he met Jude Law, then at the peak of his career: '[He came] up to me in a nightclub going, "Dan, f*****g hell, you're so lucky. What I'd give to be in your shoes and working with [Pinter]." I was looking at a multi-millionaire actor . . . asking me about Harold and envying me . . . I knew how lucky I was to be around Harold.'

There was no doubting Danny's private life was also in a very dark place, and his relationship with Davinia Taylor was about to come to an abrupt end, too. It had staggered on in a blur of drugs and alcohol, and throughout 2001 the tabloids speculated about the pair, Danny falling foul of several 'kiss and tell' stories, alleged affairs linking him to several other women. The *Sunday Mirror* reported he'd started a relationship with Billie Piper, although Danny would later insist that it was very brief, stating, 'Me and Billie did have a thing going, but it was really low-key. We were just good friends.' While many of the details about his time with Davinia remain firmly under wraps – Danny famously refused to even mention Taylor's name in his autobiography in order to show respect to Joanne – there was no doubting it was a tempestuous affair, leaving Danny physically shattered and emotionally scarred.

In the summer of 2002, Danny decided he had had enough. In the end, with little warning and no drama, he packed up what few belongings he had and moved back to his grandma's house in Stratford. While it was a long time coming, this was the next vital stepping stone in his personal (and eventually professional) recovery. He would lose a further eight months of his life in another haze of drink and drugs, but he would come out the other end stronger and finally ready to greet the next important phase: returning to film acting and becoming a bankable leading man.

Danny's focus may have been returning to film and television, but he never lost his love of stage acting and the unique challenges and rewards it brought. He would take to the stage again, in another Pinter revival – of *The Homecoming* in 2008 – as well as starring in a critically acclaimed play about Sid Vicious and Kurt Cobain entitled *Kurt and Sid* in 2009.

As for Harold Pinter, since his death in 2008, Danny has often stated how important the great playwright was to him – both as a mentor and as a friend. He sums up their relationship in *Straight Up*, saying, 'independent of my respect for the bloke . . . I think it's worth saying what his approval did for an actor. He opened me up to a whole new audience, and he brought me credibility.' In another interview in the *Guardian*, he said, 'I miss him . . . he was a f*****g tyrant . . . but he could get away with it because he was so enchanting . . . He was a good influence on me. He was the only person who I feared but loved. He had faith in me. He suffered all my s**t because he knew I was a talented actor . . . I learned so much from him that set me up for the rest of my career.'

CHAPTER EIGHT

FALLING IN LOVE AGAIN

While starring in Harold Pinter's *No Man's Land* at the National Theatre, Danny spent the first half of 2002 trying to get his disastrous private life back onto an even keel. By May, his affair with Davinia Taylor was over: it had wrung him out and left his relationship with Joanne and Dani at an all-time low.

In desperation, Danny would wait outside his old house, hoping to catch extra glimpses of his daughter as she returned from school – aside from the few times he was allowed to spend time with her – only to be blanked completely by Joanne. As always, his method of dealing with pain and rejection was to abuse his body: he drank vodka around the clock, helping jeopardize much of the headway he had made in his career over the previous decade. He had reconnected with all of his East London friends and was settling back into his old self-destructive routine. In his book, he sums it up perfectly, saying, 'I felt like a shadow in my own life.'

During this time, he was, remarkably, still getting a few job offers and, although he was not landing any major film roles, he took the work where he could get it. He added his voice to the video game *Grand Theft Auto: Vice City* and returned to television after an absence of almost five years.

Danny was not coping well with what he perceived as a dramatic decline of his clout as an actor. He saw it as a professional fall from grace and his ego took a bit of a beating as he struggled to come to terms with his lowered status within the industry. His dissatisfaction came to a head when he accepted a role in an Asian television drama, *Second Generation*, which saw him acting alongside Parminder Nagra, star of *Bend It Like Beckham*.

Danny performed most of the made-for-TV film drunk or under the influence of one drug or another. On one occasion, he even invited a couple of his friends to the set with him. Between takes, he'd return to his trailer and rejoin the party, only pulling himself together when he was needed back in front of the camera. Again, the financial restraints that exist on most productions meant he felt confident he was irreplaceable once it was up and running. He was right, but he failed to realize what his bad behaviour was doing to his reputation. It's relatively easy to avoid being sacked from a job you already have, but soon Danny would find himself considered virtually untouchable by many casting agents and directors. As with most occupations, but particularly true of acting, there's always someone coming up on your heels who is just as talented. Danny looks back at this time in *Straight Up*, saying, 'I feel truly sorry about the way I treated people back then, but I wasn't myself. I would never disrespect the other actors, the crew and the viewers like that nowadays … The only explanation I can give is that I was dying inside without my family around me.'

It's safe to assume that the phone in Danny's agent's office had not been ringing quite so frequently once stories of his drunkenness and drug use on set had begun to spread through the close-knit British television and film industry. One can imagine a state of high alert erupting when anyone did ring asking to be put in touch with him. But it was one unexpected call to his agent that would see his acting career scale heights unforeseen from his current nadir.

Danny's relationship with Nick Love – who had given Danny a much needed helping hand by casting him in his debut picture, *Goodbye Charlie Bright* – had been professionally satisfying and the pair had got on well during filming, but in real terms any friendship had all but ended after their time together on set. The film's relative financial failure had stalled Love's career as a feature director for a couple of years and he was only now in the position to start work on his second film, a warts-and-all look at the controversial subject of football hooliganism titled *The Football Factory*.

Danny was a little shocked that a call from Love had come via his agent, rather than directly from the man himself, but he dismissed any initial suspicions as Love attempting to maintain as much of a serious approach as possible. He headed to their arranged meeting, at The Groucho Club in central London, with a sense of excitement, eager to catch up with Nick and perhaps discuss any upcoming projects he had in the works.

The meeting was a short, sharp shock rather than a happy reunion. It was immediately obvious Love was not the same carefree, affectionate and encouraging man he had worked with two years ago. Love instantly pulled a script from his bag and threw it on the table in front of Danny. In *The Films of Danny Dyer*, Danny recalled Love's words: 'F*****g read that. I can't offer it to you now because you've become unreliable, and the producers don't think you're going to turn up every day.' He explained that he was willing to fight for Danny, but he would only hire him if he cleaned up his act and auditioned alongside everyone else. With that, Love left. Danny was gobsmacked, and rather than ending the night in another drink- and drug-fuelled haze, he headed home.

As he travelled back to Stratford, he was overwhelmed by a feeling of hopelessness and began to sob uncontrollably. Love had delivered the ultimate wake-up call. The emotions engulfing Danny at that precise moment – the recognition that his reputation was in tatters, coupled with the regrets about his personal situation – delivered the spark he needed to reignite the fire in his belly.

As soon as he started on the script, it hit him like an armoured truck: this was the film he had been working towards his whole professional life. Danny devoted every waking hour to reading, re-reading and dissecting it. He was determined there would be no one in the audition room more prepared than he was; they were not going to steal the role of a lifetime from under his nose.

In the end, Danny faced stiff competition from one other actor, a relative unknown by the name of Tom Hardy. Although Love had levelled the playing field, insisting the best man on the day would win the role, when it came to *The Football Factory* audition, Danny had a distinct advantage – he was working class and knew these characters inside out. He'd spent time on the football terraces; he'd grown up surrounded by the ever-present undercurrent of danger that could erupt at a moment's notice and he understood the heady mix of exaggerated masculinity, violence for violence's sake and the unquestioning loyalty you were expected to show towards your own. Hardy's parents were artists and writers and he'd received formal acting training at drama schools in London. While that might stand him in good stead later in his career, in this case it worked against him, and he failed to convince the producers that he could deliver the same raw edginess and simmering aggression Danny had shown in his audition.

Danny knew this role could be his last chance to fully realize his early potential. He had been thrown a lifeline by one of the few people who truly believed in him and knew how to snap him out of the self-destructive rut he had fallen into.

After an agonizing wait, Love called Danny and confirmed he had landed the role of Tommy Johnson, the lead character in *The Football Factory*. In his book, Danny recalled the director's typically blunt words: 'You're in, boy. You f*****g dare turn up late once, or pissed, and I will punch you in the mouth.'

For Danny, this was more than just the relief of landing his dream job; it was a chance to get back on track and validation that he still had at least a little clout as an actor. He knew his reputation had taken a battering and was determined to use *The Football Factory* as his rehab. He was painfully aware he couldn't mess this up and threw himself, heart and soul, into the job at hand. He (more or less) gave up alcohol and drugs, determined not to allow anything to distract him or lead him astray.

Danny was introduced to the other actors, including Tamer Hassan, who would play Millwall Fred in the film. Hassan owned Greenwich Borough Football Club and allowed Love to use it as a location for much of the film. He was a straight-talking South Londoner who had witnessed the Millwall football hooligan scene in his youth, and he and Danny hit it off immediately. After feeling like an outsider for so long, alienated by his working-class upbringing, Danny was eventually meeting people in the industry who shared a similar background to his and who he felt comfortable with on and off the film set – and that started with the director.

With *The Football Factory*, Love was trying to shine a light on a subject few people fully understood. Football hooliganism was not something that touched the lives of the average person, save for the odd sensational tabloid headline or shocking piece of news footage. Love wanted to explore a phenomenon that saw normal family men leave home on a Saturday afternoon, lose themselves on the terraces and in the pubs surrounding the stadiums and then return home to their wives and children for dinner.

Love bravely used several real football hooligan gangs as extras on the movie when it started shooting in April 2003. These were truly dangerous characters – as if to illustrate their involvement in the violence sometimes associated with the sport, some still had their police tags on and others were awaiting trial. Complete with their beer bellies, tattoos and missing teeth, they were what gave the finished product its unique authenticity and meant the set could be a lively and unpredictable place. Danny, always keen to be 'one of the lads' when filming, was, for him, in the unusual position of trying to keep clean and sober at work. He would hang out with the gangs, who'd turn up with their cans of beer and cannabis, but only take a sip of what they offered, pouring the rest away when they weren't looking. There was certainly a bubbling rivalry between the rival groups, but it was all carefully diverted by Love and his team of stuntmen into the film's many action-packed fight scenes.

The director's major achievement with the film was managing to translate the unexpectedly affectionate bonds between these violent men, their camaraderie and the loyalty they show one another. As with *Goodbye Charlie Bright*, the film was essentially a love story between two men – two straight men, but a love story nonetheless.

The whole experience was an unmitigated success for Danny. He was back, recharged and firing on all cylinders. He summed it up in *Straight Up*, saying, 'The film was a complete joy for me. I jumped out of bed every morning just to get on set.' Compare this to the Danny who had been struggling to even get to work just six months earlier and it's easy to see that he had finally learnt an important lesson: acting and drugs are not a good combination.

Danny had been right to put everything on the line for this film. He was a revelation in the role. His character, Tommy, feels trapped by the culture of hate and brutality he is a part of, questioning his place in a cycle of violence where danger lurks around every corner. It's a complex portrayal of a young man torn between accepting what he knows and his desire to break free from his fate, and the film saw Danny deliver his most accomplished performance yet.

Danny's enduring reputation as a hard man has its roots in this film, but he is adamant that this character, and the many that followed, couldn't be less like the real him. In his autobiography, he states, 'I don't think I've ever started a fight in my life. I'm an easy-going bloke and proud of it.'

The Football Factory would eventually be released on 14 May 2004 to modest success, turning a reasonable profit within its first few weeks. The box office may have been adversely affected, however, by an unusually large number of bootleg copies of a rough cut of the film being leaked prior to release, but many believe this was a deliberate attempt by the film-makers to build an early buzz around the film.

It worked, and the picture hit a chord among its target audience. The movie's tabloid-baiting subject matter saw it attract more than its fair share of newspaper column inches and it provoked discussions and fierce debate on the subject of football hooliganism that lasted for a long time to come.

The real legacy of the film was cemented as Danny, Nick

Love and other key members of the cast embarked on a publicity tour that saw them showing the film to confirmed football hooligans all over the country, holding question and answer sessions afterwards on their respective home turfs. Eventually becoming a cult classic on home video and DVD, the movie sparked a wave of imitators and copycat titles, but it still stands up today as the definitive big screen exploration of the football hooligan phenomenon and so-called 'thug culture'.

The film saw Danny's fan base, and the fame and attention that accompany it, increase exponentially. He had just about become used to the unique crowd that worshipped Moff, his *Human Traffic* character, but *The Football Factory*'s hardcore were something else. These were not peace-loving clubbers, they were real hard men, and an altogether much scarier crowd.

Professionally, making the movie put Danny back on top of the world. And it wouldn't be long before his personal life was similarly back on track.

His relationship with Joanne had hit rock bottom during the previous twelve months. He was still trying to be a part of his daughter's life, but was almost completely estranged from her mother. It had reached the stage where the former childhood sweethearts wouldn't even acknowledge one another when Danny turned up at Joanne's house to collect Dani. As time went on, both Danny and Joanne had started seeing other people. While Danny admits his relationships away from Joanne were mostly casual affairs, with girls who liked to party and wanted to be seen with a version of the man they recognized from the papers, he'd finally realized the only woman he really wanted to be with was Joanne, the mother of his daughter. Joanne, on the other hand, had started a more serious relationship, hoping that by moving on she could give Dani greater stability and a degree of normality in her home life. Eventually, their frosty relationship began to thaw as Danny persevered in his attempts to restart some vestige of cordiality. Danny started to feel some of the old spark the couple had shared when they first started dating back in their teens return and he was finding more and more excuses to visit Dani, while secretly hoping to spend more time with Joanne as well.

In a bizarre twist of events, the pair, who were still both involved with other people, started having an affair. They were sneaking around spending time together, until eventually they realized they were better off as a proper family, and decided to get back together. It can't have been an easy decision for Joanne, but there was no doubting Danny's sincerity, and the two reuniting was undoubtedly the best thing for their daughter.

Over the years, their relationship would hit a few more minor bumps, but from here on in, Danny was completely committed to Joanne. He told the *Mirror*, 'She is a good East End girl . . . I totally adore Joanne and I'm a lucky man.' He revealed their bond was now virtually unbreakable because they had been together since they were kids and gone through so much: 'When we [have] split up, we'd still see each other and then we realized we were meant to be . . . I love her to bits.'

During the period after completing filming on *The Football Factory*, but before it had been released in cinemas, Danny found himself rejuvenated and ready to keep working. Although word was beginning to spread about his renewed commitment and resolve to work hard, he was still not the first name on everyone's list during casting sessions and the offers of work were not flooding in.

One project from this period, however, that many of Danny's biggest fans are unlikely to have seen, was a short film called *Wasp*, which features one of his most understated and natural performances. (It's also the answer to one of the best quiz questions of all time: 'Which Danny Dyer film picked up an Oscar in 2004?') Danny had been approached on the set of *The Football Factory* with a script by a young film-maker, Andrea Arnold, who had been commissioned to make a short film by the UK Film Council and Channel 4. Danny loved the story and when he met with Arnold, they clicked immediately. He agreed to take part in the film as a favour – he was only paid £250 for his role – and was intrigued by Arnold insisting she wanted to use real working-class kids and untrained actors to fill out the rest of the cast.

Released in 2003, the film focused on the plight of a single mother with very little money and no hope of escape, trying to look after her brood of four young children. Danny played a boy who asks the girl out on a date, not realizing the kids she has with her are her own. The girl keeps this secret until the end of the film, only revealing the truth when confronted by Danny. The audience's expectations are turned on their head when Danny's character, instead of running a mile, picks up the whole family in his car and buys them all chips.

Arnold had an unusual method of casting her actors, hanging around a local estate and approaching the children she thought would work well in the film, before asking them to take her home to meet their parents. While this may seem foolhardy, it was a strategy that delivered an extremely raw and engaging set of supporting performances. The casting of the other adult role was more conventional, and the girl would be played by an up-and-coming young actress called Natalie Press.

Wasp was a simple but extremely effective piece of story-telling. Arnold's style of direction involved long, uninterrupted takes, with the actors left to improvise within the basic structure of the scene. This technique, while artistically rewarding, could be tiring for the actors – especially if they were waiting around off-camera. Danny admits his patience was wearing thin as the film's night shoots were particularly arduous for the four inexperienced kids, who grew tired and increasingly restless. But Danny soon understood the advantages of this method once he saw some of Arnold's edited early footage. She had managed to capture some startlingly visceral, intimate and completely natural moments between the children and the adult actors, giving the film a subtle, yet powerful, intensity.

It was a beautifully made film and was an instant hit on the independent film awards circuit, showing and competing at countless events. The film eventually picked up awards at the Sundance and Toronto Film Festivals before being nominated for the Best Live Action Short Film at the Academy Awards in 2004. On the night of the Oscars, Danny was out of the country filming a documentary, but had been understandably excited to see his image, in a scene from the film, being projected in front of thousands of the most famous and influential film-makers and actors in the business. The fact that the film actually won the award rounded off a unique experience for him.

After filming on *Wasp* had finished, Danny was still waiting for *The Football Factory* to be released and money, or more accurately the lack of it, was starting to become a bit more of a problem. Danny was obviously overjoyed he had managed to reunite his little family unit, but the profligate lifestyle he had been enjoying over the last couple of years with Davinia

Taylor had left him short of funds. He was now the main breadwinner again and he needed to keep working. While it was obvious he wasn't going to be heading back to labouring or temping, he needed to find new ways to make a living.

Thankfully, Nick Love had informed his regular company of actors he intended to sustain the momentum he'd built with *The Football Factory* by jumping straight into pre-production on another of his own scripts. As soon as he'd completed the final edit and promotional duties on *The Football Factory* he would be prepping a new film, *The Business*, with the intention of shooting it during the summer of 2004.

Danny refrained from taking any big jobs that might tie him up for an extended period of time, but he was able to work on a few smaller projects, the first of which was a film called *Tabloid*, which, despite boasting an impressive cast and a decent budget and a sharply observed satirical script, was never given a cinema or DVD release in the UK. For Danny, it acted as a timely reminder of the fickle nature of the film industry and proof that you can never tell where your next success, or indeed your next failure, is coming from.

The next project he committed to seemed like the perfect stopgap job. He'd received a script from a film-maker named Thomas Clay, a first-time director who planned to finance his film completely with his own money. Danny was always flattered when talented new writers and directors approached him with work and the fact he would be paid a reasonable amount for only four days' filming was a bonus. Danny's big mistake – one he would never make again – was not reading the entire script.

The movie was called *The Great Ecstasy of Robert Carmichael* and Danny's scenes only appear near the beginning of the film, and thus he didn't bother to read past that point in the script.

Starting out: Danny's early work saw him take on a variety of roles, and sport a range of looks, notably as a long-haired youth in *Cadfael* (**above**) and a disgruntled football fan in *A Touch of Frost* (**left**), both 1995.

(**Left**) Danny still appears fresh-faced as he poses with co-stars John Simm and Nicola Reynolds at the *Human Traffic* premiere in London in 1999.

(**Below**) And not quite so charming as his character from the film, Moff.

(**Above**) Looking every inch the calm, sophisticated First World War army officer in 1999's *The Trench*, Danny's character was later proved to be somewhat cowardly.

(**Right**) Danny poses with old girlfriend Davinia Taylor at *The 51st State* premiere in London.

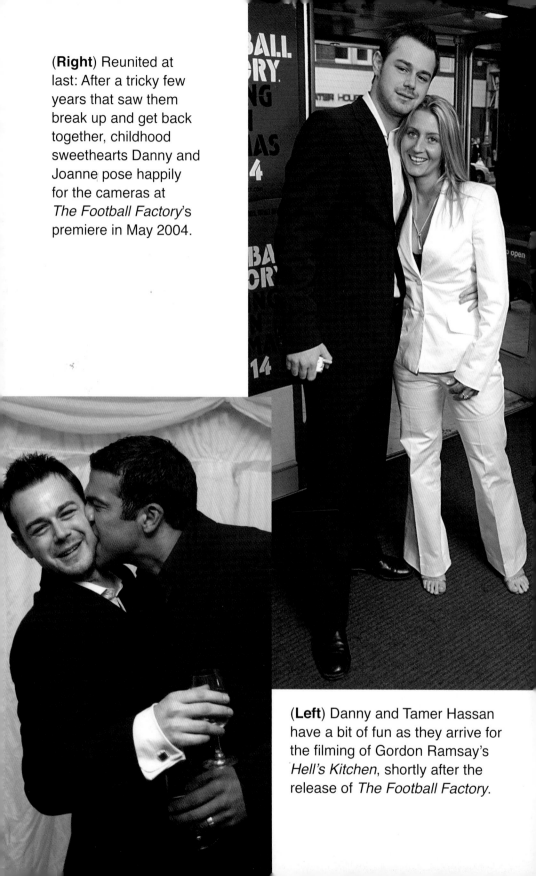

(**Right**) Reunited at last: After a tricky few years that saw them break up and get back together, childhood sweethearts Danny and Joanne pose happily for the cameras at *The Football Factory*'s premiere in May 2004.

(**Left**) Danny and Tamer Hassan have a bit of fun as they arrive for the filming of Gordon Ramsay's *Hell's Kitchen*, shortly after the release of *The Football Factory*.

(**Above**) High point: Danny is back to his best in a role written especially for him in Nick Love's *The Business*. With co-stars (*l–r*) Tamer Hassan, Georgina Chapman and Geoff Bell.

(**Below**) Looking the part in his 1980s-era outfit as Frankie on the set of *The Business*, released in 2005.

(**Above**) A departure in genre for Danny saw him feature in 2006's comedy-horror, *Severance*. With other cast members (*l–r*) Tim McInnerny, Babou Ceesay, Andy Nyman, Claudie Blakley and Laura Harris.

(**Below**) Danny poses with Laura Harris and director Christopher Smith during a photocall prior to the press presentation of *Severance*.

(**Above**) *Outlaw*, 2007, was the last installment of a remarkable collaboration between Danny and director Nick Love, and saw him team up with (*l–r*) Sean Harris, Sean Bean, Rupert Friend and Lennie James.

(**Right**) Crush: Danny was absolutely thrilled to work with Gillian Anderson in *Straightheads* in 2007. Unfortunately, at the time of writing, the movie was his last to see a wide release in UK cinemas.

Low point: Danny made a succession of unsuccessful low-budget independent movies, which started with *City Rats* in 2009 (at the London premiere with director Steve Kelly and Tamer Hassan, **above left**), and continued with what was viewed as his personal nadir, *Basement*, 2010 (**above right**), before 2011's *Age of Heroes*, for which he is seen receiving weapons training (**left**).

If he had, he would have come across some very disturbing parts of the story, featuring graphic sexual violence. When the film was shown at the Cannes Film Festival, it received an unprecedented reaction from the audience for its extreme tastelessness. Danny started to see reports of people being sick as they watched it and, as the biggest name in the cast, he received part of the blame. He admitted in his book, 'I was embarrassed to be associated with it, to be honest.' Thankfully, the quality of his work on *The Business* meant that *Robert Carmichael* survives as little more than a footnote on Danny's CV.

He also managed to squeeze another minor project into this period of Nick Love-induced limbo, a romantic comedy entitled *The Other Half*. However, the film was woefully short on both romance and comedy, but the producers were planning to use the upcoming Euro 2004 football championships as the backdrop to the film and offered Danny tickets to every England match as a sweetener to ensure his involvement.

The story saw Danny taking his new bride on honeymoon to Portugal on the pretence that it would be a beautiful holiday experience, while secretly sneaking out to every England match without her knowing this had been his intention all along.

In the end, the film turned into a bit of a fiasco. Danny had to attend the England games alone as the producers had only managed to secure one ticket for each match. It seemed most of the budget for the film had been spent on acquiring these single tickets, leaving Danny to sleep on a blow-up mattress in the apartment he had to share with the lead actress and the producer. The crew had not secured any permits to allow them to film legally and everything had to be done on the fly, which was made virtually impossible by the fact Danny was now constantly recognized as 'that guy from *The Football*

Factory'. To round the farcical experience off, the ending of the film – which was meant to involve the couple celebrating their newfound love for each other as England lifted the trophy – was scuppered by England's sharp exit from the tournament in the quarter-finals. Danny had considered jumping ship, but stayed on, buoyed by the fact England's defeat meant the filming would wrap up early. He also had to endure one day's filming with Vinnie Jones, who had been drafted in to bookend the film. Danny was not enamoured of Jones after his time on *Mean Machine*, and Jones' behaviour here – leaving to go home immediately after shooting his scenes – would do nothing to improve their relationship.

Thankfully, Nick Love had finally completed his script for *The Business* and there was a part in it created solely for Danny. The director contacted him personally, offering him the lead role. Having a part written specifically for him was a great honour for Danny, as he felt it was a real seal of approval from Love, one which he did not take for granted.

In his autobiography, he described feeling like a child on Christmas Day as he got the script. Such excitement is certainly understandable, as this was Danny's first real leading role. He was set to play Frankie, a naive wannabe London gangster who dreams of escaping the inevitable dead-end drudgery of his working-class background and making something of his life. After he is involved in a serious assault, he flees the UK and agrees to make a 'no-questions-asked' delivery to a family friend, Playboy Charlie, on the Costa del Sol. Unwittingly, Frankie has made his first drug run. Frankie and Charlie bond immediately, and the latter decides to take the young man under his wing. Over the course of the next decade, he becomes embroiled in their various illegal exploits and reaps the many rewards associated with a life of crime – money, beautiful women and power. As the gang's involvement in the Moroccan drug trade escalates, so too does Frankie's influence with them, and eventually he is enjoying the luxury lifestyle and status he has fantasized about all his life.

As with *The Football Factory*, Love was keen not to glamorize the lifestyle or the violence of the drug dealers. He wanted to make the consequences of their actions clear for both criminal and victim, and did not shy away from showing the gang's eventual downfall. As always, Love was much more interested in exploring the relationships of a group of people thrown together and living in extreme circumstances, examining how far their loyalties would stretch once tested.

Love aimed to lift the lid on the ex-pat criminal gangs operating in and around the Spanish coastal regions, hoping to do for organized crime gangs what *The Football Factory* had done for football hooliganism. The film is set in the early 1980s, at a time when Spain's Costa del Sol became a safe haven for countless fugitives, criminals and gangsters – so much so that the region was christened the Costa del Crime by the British media.

Danny was set to join Love and the rest of the crew in Spain for a week of preparation and rehearsals before filming began. After severe flight delays, Danny arrived at their Spanish hotel a little worse for wear, and unfortunately for him, the director was waiting for him in the hotel lobby and was furious when he saw how drunk his lead actor was. Thinking Danny had learnt nothing and was throwing the lifeline he'd given him back in his face, Love stormed off.

Danny was disappointed in himself, not least because he was more or less drug-free at this stage, but also because he knew worrying about the actors he had hand-picked for his film was the last thing Love needed. While it didn't exactly set the tone for the entire shoot, it acted as an early indication of the pressure Love felt filming *The Business*.

This was a big step up for Love in terms of delivering on his early promise, and he had been given a much bigger budget to work with, and consequently had to deal with the expectations that went with it. In an interview on *The Business*'s DVD extras, Love says, 'On my first film, I had to answer to people. I didn't know what I was doing. I hadn't found my aggression. I didn't really understand the game. But *The Football Factory* and *The Business*, they are both exactly the films I wanted to make.'

A perfectionist, Love expected everyone and everything to be just the way he wanted it on a film set, and with this movie in particular, he had the added complication of the 1980s period setting. He was determined every element would be authentically eighties, stating on the DVD, 'You can't afford to be wrong. You just can't get one thing wrong or it will scupper someone's enjoyment of the film.' This preoccupation with capturing the detail, or, as Love himself describes it, the 'camp and cool' nature of the decade, would cause several problems with the film's production designers and set dressers. As a result, the atmosphere on set was decidedly more tense and aggressive than Danny was used to – and, considering Love's last picture saw drunken football hooligans on the production, that was saying something.

Littered with minute details, the film flawlessly captures the look and feel of the era. From Adidas supplying vintage trainers for the actors to wear to the costume department sourcing original designer gear and clothes from extinct fashion labels, everything looks real. Love would veto certain branded shopping bags appearing in a shot if he was unsure about their authenticity and double-checked every bottle on display behind the bar in the nightclub scenes to ensure it belonged there. The film's colour palette changes from dull, washed-out greys in the sequences set in England to the bold, over-saturated colours and DayGlo highlights used to signify the hedonistic extravagance of the Spanish lifestyle. Add a soundtrack featuring some of the biggest eighties hits (and a few lesser-known cult classics), and Love succeeded in creating a perfect, nostalgic snapshot of the decade.

Danny's preparation, on the other hand, was minimal. Love was well aware of what Danny could deliver, but wanted him to understand the idea of 'honour among thieves' and get to grips with the relationships that exist between men who are bound to one another more by necessity than love. He needed him to see how mutual distrust and the fear of betrayal can create stronger bonds than friendship. He had asked Danny to watch Martin Scorsese's *Goodfellas* and *The Godfather* trilogy to get an understanding of one of the main themes of his film, in the latter paying particular attention to the journey Al Pacino's character makes as he rises through the ranks of the Mob towards his ultimate fate.

After getting off on the wrong foot with Love on the film, things for Danny improved once they started filming. The director had shown a lot of faith in him, giving him the lead role in his biggest film to date, and Danny was not only relishing the opportunity to work with Love again, but was also glad to reconnect with Tamer Hassan and his old *Charlie Bright* and *Football Factory* co-star, Roland Manookian. The fact that the movie had been custom-written for the actors, using Love's familiarity with their past performances, nurtured an almost telepathic understanding between the group of actors and the director.

This meant the mood changed from tense to extremely focused very quickly. That feeling of being totally wrapped up in their characters wasn't left on set; Danny recalls he and the principal actors would head back to the hotel after the day's work and talk obsessively about their characters and their relationships well into the early hours. This total immersion in their roles would continue for over two months of shooting.

It was an intoxicating, creative atmosphere for Danny and, as he revealed in an interview for DVD, one which had its positives and negatives. '[I've got] a lot on my mind. The hardest thing for me is shaking it off at the end of the day because my [head's] all over the place at the moment. I'm so involved with this job. I'm obsessed with it, which is great when you're filming but [not so much] when you go home.' He added, 'I'm learning a lot as an actor because I've never been that involved in a part; I've never had the opportunity to [employ this] method.'

As part of his extra responsibility on the film, Love allowed Danny to take part in the casting process for the main female character, and he was only too happy to sit in on the auditions of countless beautiful girls to test their on-screen chemistry. The eventual choice of Georgina Chapman in the role may not have been the best choice, as the lack of a spark between Danny and Chapman is clearly visible in the finished cut.

It is probably just as well that his leading lady was less of a distraction than she might have been, as a large contingent of the Dyer family had been invited along for some of the location shoot. Perhaps conscious of what had happened on Danny's last extended movie abroad, Joanne and Dani, as well as Danny's mother, grandma and sister, all spent some holiday time with him while he was filming in Spain. Being able to show off a little and treating his family was one of the many highlights of the experience.

Principal photography continued well into October 2004,

with additional location footage shot back in the UK for the opening scenes and flashbacks. When filming was over, there was a long and exhaustive process to get the picture ready for official release. Love, speaking in an interview on the DVD, said, 'There's not a single person in the cast that has [given] anything less than 100 per cent, I love it.' In extracting yet another uninhibited and well-balanced performance from Danny, Love had demonstrated that their ongoing collaboration was an increasingly fruitful one.

With the finished film in the can, it seemed the intensity and passion everyone had expended on the project was paying off. Love in particular received praise upon its release in September 2005, with Adrian Hennigan in his review for the BBC Film website proclaiming, 'Nick Love is now officially Britain's hottest director.'

The movie was yet another entry in Love's study of the complexity of male relationships, something he'd continue to explore in his work, including in his last release, *The Sweeney*, in 2012. But with *The Business*, Love was also reaching for something more layered and textured. The film has obvious thematic links to the Hollywood gangster films of the 1930s, but Love, through his choice of locations and shooting style, also wanted to conjure images of the Wild West, and in particular the spaghetti Westerns of Sergio Leone. The lawlessness and unrestricted violence meted out by the ex-pat gangsters, as well as their corruption and exploitation of the Spanish locals, acts as a decent metaphor for the colonization of the American Old West.

The Business was fairly well received by UK critics upon its release in 2005, Jason Solomons labelling it 'deliciously entertaining' in his *Observer* review, while *NME* branded it 'a gangster gem'. The film fared best with the 'lads' mags', which took the mix of gangsters, guns and girls to their hearts. Here was a film that spoke their language, *Nuts* calling it 'savagely funny' and awarding it five stars, and Jeff Maysh at *Loaded* matching the rating, writing, 'finally, a blindin' British gangster film'. *Front* raved the film had 'more guns than Goodfellas, more charlie than Casino and more swearing than Scarface'. The movie also performed at the UK box office, turning a profit on its release and becoming a sizeable hit on DVD, having sold around a million copies at the time of writing.

There is little doubt the film stands up today as a high point in Danny's career. His director, Nick Love, revealed during the 'making of' documentary for the film, 'He's got this amazing stillness [that proved] to be priceless on this film', and told Film4 that 'most of the stuff was done in just one or two takes'. Danny, in *The Films of Danny Dyer*, agreed it was a quality piece of work, saying, 'I'm so proud of *The Business* . . . I'm really happy I'm in it. I'm so on it in that film.' He finished, 'It set me up nicely for whatever I was going to do next.'

As it turned out, *The Business* would be the only time Nick Love would write a role specifically for Danny, and, as such, the film is still the pair's masterpiece. Their relationship had been extremely productive and had allowed both director and actor to reach new heights in their professional lives. In the intervening years, however, Love has struggled to recapture the promise evident in his early work and has only made three movies since filming *The Business*. Today, Danny's relationship with Love has petered out and it remains to be seen if the director will find another suitably inspirational muse for his work. But for Danny, back in 2005, their collaboration was not yet over, and elsewhere, things were looking up.

MTV contacted Danny about an idea they had for a documentary called *The Backpacker's Guide to Thailand*, which would follow a British backpacker travelling around the country, witnessing first hand the devastation left behind by the tsunami that hit on 26 December 2004. They hoped the awareness from the piece might help kick-start the country's shattered economy, which had relied so heavily on the tourist trade. Danny needed the money and, relishing the thought of a free holiday, agreed to head out to Thailand in February 2005. He admits that he wasn't really thinking about what he was about to see, yet, even so, nothing could have prepared him for the reality of the situation.

MTV eased Danny into the job by taking him around a few of the inland tourist destinations, but it wasn't long before he was confronted with the full force of what had happened only a few weeks before. He interviewed survivors who had faced the total destruction of everything they owned and met many who had seen the deaths of their entire families. Soon he was helping the aid workers and locals as they searched for bodies, hoping that DNA testing would assist in identifying as many of the deceased as possible. Danny was as unaware as most of the viewers back home as to what had happened to the country after the news crews left the scene, and it made for heartbreaking viewing. He was deeply affected by his experiences there and felt it changed him in ways that were impossible to describe; watching his distress and astonishment as he reacted to what he saw around him was genuinely moving, and all too real. Danny began to think about Joanne and Dani back home, appreciating what it would mean to lose something so precious. As a tribute to the people he'd met and as a constant reminder of what was most important in his life he decided to get Dani's name tattooed on his hand – he'd never again undervalue what was most precious to him.

Next up for Danny would be a comedy horror film called

Severance. The mastermind behind the film was relative newcomer Christopher Smith. Smith's debut feature, *Creep*, had wowed critics and become a cult hit with both British and American audiences. For his follow-up, Smith wanted to use real locations and ramp up the humour, as well as the horror elements. The film saw Danny play another version of his drug-obsessed, pill-popping persona, perfected in *Human Traffic*. He would be one of a group of co-workers sent on a team-building weekend by their employer. The group get lost on the way to their hotel and end up staying at a disused research facility, and are soon being picked off, one by one, by the human experiments that have been abandoned there.

Getting the part had been an unusual struggle for Danny. The producers were sure Danny could handle the action and the physical side of the performance, but had doubts about his ability to deliver on the comedy elements of the script, wrongly assuming his range was limited to hard men and hooligans. Director Smith made sure they saw *Human Traffic*, which eventually helped swing the decision Danny's way. Danny headed off to Hungary with a spring in his step: he was about to play his first action hero role – be it one with a shotgun in one hand and a joint in the other!

Joanne needn't have worried about Danny going on another long shoot abroad: he was in a particularly good place as far as drink and drugs were concerned, and while he was never going to be a 100 per cent teetotal or completely drug-free, he had really cleaned up his act and seemed to have finally learned his lesson. Even without a set visit from Joanne or his family, Danny remained totally focused on the work during the *Severance* shoot, acting the consummate professional.

Danny admired Smith's directing style, which mirrored the energy and enthusiasm of Nick Love, but without any of the latter's aggressive tendencies. The atmosphere on set was intense: there was a lot to be done in a relatively short time, but this did not lessen the banter between cast and crew, which remained light-hearted, and Danny was relishing the opportunity to show off some of his underused comedic talents. In an on-set interview, later used as part of the DVD bonus material, Danny said he was disappointed he'd had to rein in his bad language in order to make sure the film secured a 15 certificate, joking, 'It cuts my range down a little bit.'

It was a long and complicated shoot, however. Multiple practical special-effects sequences meant lots of waiting around between takes, and the horrific wounds needed for a horror movie required most of the cast to spend hours in the make-up chair.

Danny was again struggling to cope with being away from Joanne and Dani for an extended period of time, and after a month in the Hungarian wilderness, the whole crew moved to a new base camp on the Isle of Man. Here, they would spend the rest of the production capturing exterior shots and filming all the interiors on a specially built set. Hungary had felt a long way away from his family and Danny recalled on the film's DVD extras, 'I couldn't wait to leave it. I didn't think I'd ever, ever find myself saying I cannot wait to get to the Isle of Man, but I did say that a few times.' Still isolated from Joanne on the new location, some of his frustration came to a head during a publicity interview for the film. Danny had complained he had found the Isle of Man depressing and unintentionally insulted the islanders. The fallout caused major problems for Danny and his agent, who was quick to remind him the Isle of Man was now a hub for film-makers and he might just find himself working there again in the future – facing crowds of angry Manx. Danny apologized in the press, but it wouldn't be the last time he'd speak before thinking things through.

The rest of the shoot was fairly uneventful and it turned out to be another extremely pleasurable experience for Danny. Speaking in commentary for the DVD, he said, 'I'm so glad it's in the can . . . [I] absolutely enjoyed every second of it, to be honest. It's been tough, it's been draining, but in the right way . . . I'm very excited about what it's going to look like.'

Owing more than a small debt to similarly unique twists on the horror genre, such as Eli Roth's *Hostel*, released the year before, *Severance* managed to successfully bridge the gap between horror and comedy, and found a decent audience in the UK on its release in August 2006, eventually becoming a sizeable hit on DVD. The film even picked up several positive reviews in the US, including from *Rolling Stone* critic Peter Travers, who wrote, 'The jolts are juicy and so are the jokes . . . Director and co-writer Christopher Smith, mischievously blending *The Office* with *Friday the 13th*, keeps things fierce and funny.'

Thanks to the success of his recent output, Danny was now considerably more famous, and his brand as a straight-talking everyman had put him on the radar of countless film and television producers, as well as commercial companies keen on employing his cross-market potential. He and Tamer Hassan became ambassadors for sportswear maker Fila after the brand's heavy exposure in *The Business* and Danny would notoriously lend his name to a magazine column in the mens' magazine, *Zoo*. So when he was approached by the Bravo TV network in 2006 to front a series of documentaries they were planning to make under the banner *The Real Football Factories*, it made perfect sense. Having Danny's name attached to the show would mean his ever-growing fan base – and Bravo's target audience – would be more likely to tune in. The money on offer was not to be sniffed at and Danny, despite having no experience in presenting, jumped at the chance.

He found the whole experience fairly soul-destroying, telling Sothcott and Mullinger in their book, 'I watch some of those documentaries and I cringe a bit.' He added that the general public overestimate the financial rewards that go along with making films, saying, 'Ultimately, I couldn't turn the money down. It wasn't a journalistic thing – I never wanted to be a presenter . . . If I could change things, I probably would.' Considering what came later, and further ill-informed involvements presenting documentaries, it is no surprise.

The series saw Danny meet groups of football hooligans from different areas of the country and even followed the English fans as they travelled abroad to overseas tournaments. It was car-crash television in a sense, but it didn't hurt Danny's reputation among his core fans – they lapped it up. However, it seemed to some in the film and television industry that Danny was mimicking his on-screen characters in real life, which unfortunately lessened his credibility in their eyes, but worse than that, it diverted attention from the strength of his recent performances and jeopardized his long-held ambitions to be taken seriously as an actor.

Danny would later go on to make a couple of similarly themed series for Bravo in 2008 and 2009 respectively, *Danny Dyer's Deadliest Men* and *Deadliest Men 2: Living Dangerously*, which only compounded people's opinions of him.

Luckily, Danny's next project in 2006 would see him back in his comfort zone in the skilful hands of Nick Love, someone who understood what Danny was capable of and was willing to give him the chance to show it. While *Outlaw* would see him returning to work with his favourite director, it wouldn't all be plain sailing and the experience was nowhere near as harmonious as their previous collaborations.

Danny goes to great lengths to stress that, despite what people might think, he has never purposely gone out of his way to stir up controversy. On the other hand, he does admit that he would never back away from it if it does come his way. In an interview in the *Independent*, in what might seem like a bit of an understatement, Danny acknowledged that some of the films he'd starred in have caused argument, stating, 'I love being part of a controversy, because it leads to debate. It gets people to think about things. I would hate the idea of making a film and people saying, "Oh, it's alright." I'd rather it upset a few people.'

From the outset, it was obvious that *Outlaw* would create a stir, with it seeming to condone vigilante justice. In the end, it was more a maelstrom than merely a stir, as the debate about the film got out of hand.

A bone of contention for Danny was the fact Love had decided to drop virtually all of his regular actors in favour of hiring some bigger names – out went Tamer Hassan and Roland Manookian, and in came Sean Bean and Bob Hoskins. Danny was approached to play a relatively small part, a deranged and racist nail bomber, and he was inclined to accept, seeing the character as a good chance to test himself and shine in a secondary role. He was still keen to stay on the good side of Hassan and the rest of his erstwhile Nick Love acting family, and thought taking a smaller part might not be seen as such an act of betrayal by them. However, Love changed his mind and asked Danny to take on a larger role, as the story's more straightforward, relatable everyman character, with his old part going to Sean Harris.

Outlaw is, on the face of it, a simple vigilante thriller that aims to explore what happens when an individual senses no one is listening and feels they have to take the law into their own hands. Sean Bean's character is a returning soldier who finds his hometown of London becoming more of a war zone than the Afghan battlefield he has just left behind, riddled with crime and violence. He recruits a band of similarly minded men and starts his own army, vowing to deliver his own brand of law enforcement and justice.

On the whole, the filming went without a hitch. Danny was excited to meet one of his idols – the star of one of his favourite movies, *The Long Good Friday* – and seeing Bob Hoskins at work, on one of his last movies before his illness-induced retirement, was a thrill. Unfortunately, Danny thought the old cliché about 'never meeting your idols' was about to come true. Initially, he found Hoskins difficult to talk to and was disappointed when the actor seemed to have no interest in football – England were valiantly battling their way through the World Cup at the time – and he worried Hoskins was struggling to fully accept the harsher elements of the script. He needn't have been concerned, though, as when Hoskins finally hit his stride, Danny was suitably impressed with the great man's work and was won over all over again.

In its transition to the big screen, the film had lost some of the more interesting and unique elements contained in the original script and there is a real sense that Love had lost his way during the editing process. In Sothcott and Mullinger's book, Danny explains, 'Nick made changes and f****d around with *Outlaw* . . . I don't think the final product was the film that he had wanted to make.' Love had lost his bullishness and unquestioning faith in his own abilities and the film would suffer as a consequence of his own second-guessing. On its release in March 2007, *Empire* praised the director's previous body of work before slating *Outlaw* in a blistering one-star review: 'Love portrays violent vigilantism as heroism . . . It's a volatile set-up with interesting questions to answer, but quickly descends into a sickening sludge of childish politics, brutality and creative swearing.' Similarly, the *Guardian* defended Love as a director, saying, 'Nick Love is still a real film-maker', before acknowledging, '*Outlaw* is crude and dull and just horrible'.

Much of the controversy ignited by the film's violent – and often, senseless – content on its initial release had just about died down when the film came out on DVD. Unfortunately for Danny, his DVD commentary, recorded with Love, was picked up by the newspapers. An edited 'highlights' video went viral on YouTube and the pair's most outlandish remarks, taken completely out of context, seemed ill judged. Danny's only defence was the fact that DVD commentaries are an odd thing to have to do, and he and Love had used the opportunity to have a laugh and say the most obscure things they could think of. The result was a prolonged barrage of swearing and banter that had little or nothing to do with the film. The fallout from this would see Danny's relationship with Love begin to deteriorate, the final nail in the coffin being Love's response to Danny's *Real Football Factories* and *Deadliest Men* documentary series.

The Real Football Factories began airing during the filming of *Outlaw* in 2006 and it is unclear whether Love even knew they existed when he hired Danny for the film. What was clear was his disapproval, as he believed Danny was cheapening himself by doing them. Love, in a 2009 interview with *Loaded* magazine, described the circumstances surrounding Danny's absence from his next film, *The Firm*, by saying, 'No way. There was never a chance; I said to him there was no way'. He explained, 'there has been a backlash against Danny. The tide has turned . . . Danny's become bigger now because of the not-so-good stuff he's done. The telly, the reality stuff. Danny knows this, I've told him.'

Danny was obviously upset by this, but also recognized that there was some truth in Love's comments. Danny's only real objection to them was why the director's personal opinion of him should so dramatically affect their working relationship. In truth, he was happy to let *The Firm* pass him by – it was another football hooligan film and he wanted to avoid revisiting similar roles to avoid people perceiving him as one kind of character. But in 2009, when Love was first hired to make a film adaptation of seventies cop show *The Sweeney*, Danny was convinced he would have been perfect to star alongside Ray Winstone in a part that eventually went to the singer Plan B. He was upset to find his relationship with Love had faded so completely and it seems he was never really considered for the part.

At this point, in 2007, Danny had always been adamant money was never his main motivation for working, but 'mates' rates' projects for Love and low-salary stage work was not going to keep Danny and his family afloat – he just wished critics, and disappointingly in this instance, Nick Love, could understand this. In *The Films of Danny Dyer*, he admits, 'In a way [taking easy jobs] was a sell-out. I gave away "me". Tom Hardy isn't going to do that. Fassbender isn't going to do that. I gave "me" away and I think I became a bit of a parody in some people's eyes.'

It was this selling of his personal brand, the inevitable controversies that sprang up around his films, as well as the countless interview gaffs Danny was prone to make, which increasingly drew focus away from his work. His next project would only add to the problem. *Straightheads*, despite featuring a very strong performance from Danny, would be one of his last films to date to receive a mainstream cinema release and it would kick-start a seemingly unstoppable decline in the quality of roles Danny would be offered over the next five or six years.

CHAPTER NINE

JUST FOR THE MONEY

Straightheads came to Danny at a time when his relationship with Nick Love appeared to be floundering and his chances of working with a similarly driven and creative director seemed unlikely. He sums up his position bluntly and concisely in the film's commentary, saying, 'I'm not in the position to pick and choose my roles, so whatever comes in front of me, I do it.'

While this approach didn't always have a positive outcome, with *Straightheads*, and in the capable hands of writer and director Dan Reed, Danny had landed on his feet.

Although *Straightheads* was his first attempt at writing and directing a feature film, Reed was something of a veteran, having fifteen years' experience as a documentary film-maker under his belt. He had spent many years studying conflict in various volatile and politically unsettled places around the world, and *Straightheads* was viewed as an exploration of what might happen if that level of violence were to enter our supposedly safe and civilized society.

Gillian Anderson was set to play Alice, a successful, independent businesswoman who becomes involved in a crazed revenge plot after she is sexually assaulted by a group of men who find her stranded in isolated woodland after a car accident. Anderson had found worldwide fame as Agent

Dana Scully in the long-running science fiction series, *The X-Files*. Although the show had also spawned a couple of movies, Anderson had so far failed to establish herself as a bankable film actress, and this was her next attempt at big-screen success.

She had already been cast when Danny was asked to audition for the role of Adam, a tradesman working on Alice's home, who becomes her lover and accomplice in her pursuit of justice through violence. The scenes Danny was sent for his first meeting with Anderson and his director, Reed, were surprisingly intimate, and Danny joked in an interview for the DVD, 'I was quite looking forward to this audition, for once'. He explained the method in a more direct approach they decided to take: 'Apparently, the other actors they saw were a bit lost and didn't really take control and that's what they wanted to see from me, for me to take control of the scene and command it a bit . . . they liked that in me. They liked that I was game and was up for it.'

Danny was aware that their acting styles couldn't be more different, but he relished the challenge of going toe-to-toe with an incredibly talented and fearless actress of Anderson's stature. Reed also saw the benefits, saying, 'It's a tremendous challenge for Danny, but it gives him something very clear to play with and lean on.'

Reed saw an unmistakable chemistry between his two actors in their initial screen-test, which was just as well, because the couple shared a lot of intimate and sexual scenes in the script. Although he accepted the offer of the role, Danny was torn by the amount of sexual content, happy that it was *the* Gillian Anderson, someone he had quite a crush on, but conscious Joanne was never particularly happy when Danny had this kind of scene in a film. He said during an on-set interview,

'It's really weird to have a licence to kiss somebody else, to be naughty with somebody else'. He then joked, 'I know my old woman's not very happy at the moment, she's got the hump ... she don't mind spending my dough, so she's got to understand how I earn it.'

It is another revelatory performance from Danny, playing slightly against type as someone out of his depth, naive and unsure of himself, but who digs deep to show courage and determination in some extremely violent situations. Anderson praised Danny's ability to capture the two sides of the character, believing he played Adam as 'observant and voyeuristic . . . shy, yet definitely able to have a good time and get what he wants'. She finished, 'He's playing that innocence and lost child [thing] very well.' Dan Reed was even more forthcoming with his praise for Danny, 'He's a very confident guy in his own right, he's completely unafraid; he's interested in his own internal logic of his own character. He's having tremendous fun.' He illustrated perfectly where Danny's level was at that particular time: 'I've seen [Danny] in a number of films and I think he is evolving as an actor. He's moving on tremendously, more focused, more concentrated, very disciplined, very constant . . . I think he's going to go far and we've caught him at the right point.'

Unfortunately, when it was released in 2007, the film failed to find much of an audience in UK or US cinemas, where it was renamed *Closure*. Ending the film with Adam's desperate acts of violent retribution was perhaps a mistake, and an earlier scene, where Alice drives off with the daughter of the man who attacked her, may have been a more suitable last shot. Whatever the reason for the choice, it would be a bitter blow for everyone involved – but probably most damaging for Danny.

Straightheads was another turning point in Danny's career. Its relative failure at the UK box office saw him slip further from the mainstream, pushing him deeper into the murkier world of independent film-making, private financing, straight-to-DVD features and micro-budget genre features. Any fantasy held by the general public about film-making being a world filled with glamour and huge financial rewards would be quickly shattered if they saw the reality of working in low-budget movies.

It was a long way down for Danny, but it is fair to say he only had himself to blame for much of what happened to his career over the next few years, given the choices he made.

He had acquired an American agent following his work on *Severance*. Everyone around him assumed *Straightheads* would help open a few doors for him internationally, and a trip to America was planned to test the waters for a possible move into bigger Hollywood movies or US television work. He told the Female First website, 'If you go to America, you will end up one of two things – either f*****g rich or a nervous wreck – but you won't know unless you go.' In the end, the trip to the US turned out to be largely fruitless. Both his agent and his management team had been confident and enthusiastic about the trip – Danny even told Hunger TV at the time, 'I've definitely got to go out there and have a crack', but in truth, his heart wasn't in it. It was another three weeks away from Joanne and his family, and he felt completely at odds with the lifestyle and the political game one is expected to play to survive in the industry over there. Danny told *Total Film* magazine that he'd met with producers in Los Angeles to talk about a role in *Wanted*, the graphic novel turned action movie that eventually starred Angelina Jolie and James McAvoy. He revealed, 'The meeting was in a restaurant and I felt it was all about the food I was ordering, the conversation we had, instead of just giving me the script and letting me read.' He continued, 'I felt vulnerable. I struggled with the fakeness', admitting, 'My American agent was ringing me and I wouldn't get back to him. He started to get a bit f****d off with it.' While he may have squandered a potentially life-changing opportunity, it seems Danny wasn't really ready to make such a transition, and certainly not without Joanne and his family.

This attempt at career progression was no doubt further scuppered by Danny's inability to completely embrace different accents in his roles, something that contributed to his perceived dependence on playing different aspects of his own personality. Danny was philosophical about it, telling LoveFilm.com, 'So I have a cockney accent, it's not all about accents; just because you can do accents, it doesn't make you a chameleon.'

Danny discussed his perceived limitations, confiding in the Sick Chirpse website, 'I would be the first to admit that I play myself in movies ... that's what I do. I pick out the best parts of my own character', adding, 'Nobody can play me better than me.' While it's true Danny has an uncanny ability to project elements of his own personality onto the screen, he is doing himself a massive disservice by branding one of his greatest assets a flaw and perpetrating a crippling misconception that sees him repeatedly underestimated as an actor, consistently labelled as someone with no real desire to challenge himself. On screen, Danny has a quality that a lot of the great actors from Hollywood's golden era possessed and one which allowed them to project their own persona onto virtually any character. Danny recognizes this ability, saying, 'I like to [paint] myself as an old school movie star because that's what they used to do years ago.'

Casting any film or television project is extremely difficult. Casting agents, like everyone else in the industry, are keen to stick to a formula that works and hire people they already know can deliver. Danny had helped create a niche for himself, but it would soon become a trap.

He had managed to salvage some of his reputation as a reliable and hard-working actor from his earlier drug and drink-dependent days. His public profile was now at an all-time high, but unfortunately the accompanying media persona, created in the tabloids and nurtured by Danny himself, didn't help him win any new friends in the industry. Yet again, Danny was finding it hard to drum up interest from producers and directors, failing to attract the kind of jobs he found interesting and, perhaps more importantly, also paid a reasonable wage.

During this period, a recommendation from Gillian Anderson meant Danny got the chance to work alongside one of his all-time acting heroes, Ray Winstone. Playing his son in a made-for-television drama called *All in the Game*, Danny relished the chance to go up against his idol. Winstone was not quick to massage the ego of any actor he was working alongside, but he and Danny gelled well together, and the latter recounted in his autobiography, '[We] hit it off immediately, like we'd known each other for years'. He told Hunger TV, 'He is still brilliant ... He said to me, "Cor, you're a blinding little actor." I wanted to sob my heart out'. With the solid working and personal relationships he enjoyed with both Winstone and Nick Love, it must have been doubly crushing for Danny to discover he wasn't even in the running for a role in Love's *The Sweeney* a few years later.

He had accepted bit parts on various television dramas, but nothing challenged him the way Nick Love's projects had. The nearest he would come to such a test was a small role in Noel Clarke's acclaimed film *Adulthood*, but even this memorable turn wasn't enough to revitalize his diminished status and re-establish him as a leading man in mainstream movies.

In truth, Danny was not working nearly as much as he would have liked and there would be a particularly quiet couple of years for him professionally following *Straightheads*, but thankfully, he had plenty to keep him busy at home.

April 2007 had seen the birth of Danny's second child, another daughter, named Sunnie, and, with a growing family, Danny was more than happy to help Joanne at home, content to be more of a presence during the first few months of Sunnie's life than he had been for Dani.

Danny and Joanne had strengthened and stabilized as a couple in the years following their separation and subsequent reconciliation, but Sunnie's birth had put extra strain on their young family. Despite earning a decent enough amount of money over the previous few years, Danny was not living an extravagant lifestyle. He had bought himself a couple of flash cars (a Porsche and a Mercedes A-Class), and Joanne and the girls wanted for nothing, but he had been reluctant to leave the small house he and Joanne still shared near the estate where they'd grown up. With only two bedrooms, he found himself sleeping on the couch downstairs, while Joanne and the baby slept in their room and Dani, now fast approaching her teens, needed the other bedroom to herself. The cramped living conditions certainly didn't improve the situation between Danny and Joanne: they were arguing a lot and the mood in the Dyer household was nearly always tense.

With very few interesting TV or film jobs coming his way, and accepting that the situation could not carry on forever, Danny agreed to star in another Pinter role, in a revival of his

1964 play, *The Homecoming*, which was set to run for the first few months of 2008. Luckily for Danny, he was able to channel all the stress and frustration he was feeling about his career and home life into the part, and he delivered another solid and praiseworthy performance. While the run was successful and well reviewed, it was the same old story of regular work, but minimal pay.

Towards the end of the *Homecoming* run, Danny and Joanne were asked to appear on an episode of the ITV quiz show *All Star Mr & Mrs*. While it wasn't something Danny was particularly interested in doing, it raised money for charity and Joanne was keen to be involved. Interviewed on *Loose Women* some time afterwards, he admitted, 'I came unstuck', explaining, '[It's] not a good idea to test your relationship live on telly . . . it was a wrong move . . . we came last'. Any suggestion of domestic bliss apparent during the recording of the show and any points Danny may have received from Joanne for doing it were quickly forgotten when a few days later, Danny agreed to join Lily Allen as a guest on her BBC Three chat show, *Lily Allen and Friends*. Filmed immediately after the play's run had ended that year, Danny was in the mood to celebrate, and a night on the town with his old friend Lily seemed to fit the bill.

Danny had known Lily Allen from her early teens through her father, Keith, with whom he starred alongside in Pinter's *Celebration* almost a decade before, and over the years they had become good friends. Their argumentative natures, relationships with alcohol and drugs and propensity for faux pas in the press made them perfect playmates.

Lily Allen and Friends was reaching the end of its first series and it seemed only natural that she would invite Danny onto the last episode as a special guest, and soon after recording finished, the pair headed out to celebrate. Unfortunately for

Danny, things escalated and the *Sun* reported he ended up on the end of Joanne's wrath, writing '[Danny has] been booted out by his missus after going on a wild bender', while they quoted a 'friend', who confirmed the story: 'Joanne's livid ... She couldn't get hold of him for three whole days after he filmed Lily's show. She knows he was with Lily and drag queen Jodie Harsh.' It's highly unlikely Danny had any sort of untoward relationship with Lily – she was just a good friend – but, nonetheless, he spent a short while sleeping back at his mother's house with the tabloids reporting he had cheated on Joanne yet again. He would be in his partner's bad graces for a while, admitting to the Digital Spy website, 'I got caught out doing something I shouldn't have done. I hate myself for what I did and for being tempted by forbidden fruit.' Joanne accepted Danny was sorry and soon relented, letting him back into the family home. Perhaps this was the final bargaining chip Joanne needed to make her case about the family's living arrangements.

Joanne was adamant the family needed to move into a bigger house and Danny, realizing he had to finally accept the inevitable and eager to keep the peace at home, reluctantly agreed to move.

Despite having worked consistently for years, Danny would need to get a mortgage like everybody else. Bizarrely, this turned out to be harder than he thought and the subsequent struggles to raise the funds forced him to finally get his financial affairs in order. Danny got his first credit card – although it's hard to believe, considering his lifestyle, he'd never found any use for one in the past – and started to think a bit more seriously about his future and the future of his family.

Danny's continued determination to work might be explained by his determination to prove something to Joanne and to give his children a better start in life than he had growing up. Danny's unwavering commitment to his family is possibly best demonstrated by the fact he decided it would be best to send his eldest daughter, Dani, to a private school rather than their local comprehensive, which he felt was not the best place for his daughter to receive her education. While it may seem at odds with a man so fiercely proud of his working-class roots, who frequently defends his hometown and champions London's East End, it shows he is also being realistic about the shortcomings of the area. Although money was never his motivation for working, for the first time in his career, Danny was forced to focus solely on just that: the figure on offer, rather than the quality of the work.

With this in mind and with a heavy heart, Danny accepted Bravo's offer to front another reality documentary series in 2008 – this time focusing on a motley selection of infamous hard men, gangsters and organized crime bosses. It was this series, entitled *Danny Dyer's Deadliest Men*, and its follow-up, *Deadliest Men 2: Living Dangerously*, which would, on the face of it, bring about the end of Danny's working relationship with Nick Love and go a long way towards irreparably destroying Danny's reputation as a serious actor. While the two documentaries might not have harmed the image his fans had of him, in certain circles these shows reinforced the feeling that Danny had become a parody of himself, trapped in a clichéd hard-man persona of his own making. He became a bit of a laughing stock, his presenting work damaging his credibility and turning some members of the film-making community off him.

Later, an attempt at a more 'serious' subject – visitors from outer space and alien abductions – in a 2010 BBC3 documentary entitled *I Believe in UFOs* only made Danny even more of a target for ridicule. To this day, he is philosophical about the choices he has been forced to make during certain periods of his career, and stresses the balance between retaining his credibility and providing for his family is a difficult one to achieve. He told Hunger TV in 2010, 'I had to go off the track and make these mad documentaries about hooligans and deadliest men, and I got a bad reputation from that. When I watch some of the shows back, I cringe.' But he was adamant he had little choice: 'It would have been great to be able to stick to acting, but unfortunately the reality is that these are the gigs that got me the house and helped me put my kids through private school.'

Years later, Danny was still haunted by questions about the work he'd done on the *Deadliest Men* documentaries. Discussing this period with Total Film in 2013, he clearly resents having to justify his decision to keep working when his chosen profession is famous for its long periods of unemployment: 'I despised it ... But I was living on a council estate still. They offered me so much money I couldn't believe it. Six figures for six weeks' work ... I've got kids. It got us a house.' Danny cites one of his acting heroes as a good precedent. 'Look at Michael Caine. Back in the eighties he was known for making terrible films, and now he's been knighted off.' He finished jokingly, 'You can only hope . . . ' While Sir Danny Dyer might still be a long way off, there's no denying he makes a fair point. Caine himself, on the occasion of his eightieth birthday, was reported in the *Telegraph* to have wholeheartedly embraced some of the undeniable stinkers on his CV. He said of 1987's *Jaws: The Revenge* (the third, and last sequel to Spielberg's original), 'I have never seen it. By all accounts it is terrible.' He added wryly, 'However, I have seen the house that it built, and it is terrific.'

It seemed Danny would need a thick skin in this period

of his working life, and his desire to survive forced him to grow one very quickly. There is no doubt he had all but lost the credibility he'd garnered through his work with Pinter and his film collaborations with Nick Love, owing in large part to the television documentaries that had now made him the butt of endless jokes and comedy parodies. Add to this his good-natured willingness to do favours for people in the industry, and he had disastrously diluted the quality of work he was being offered. Although his drive to keep working and provide for his growing family is undeniably commendable, it had led him to make some questionable choices and saw him attached to too many low-budget projects unworthy of his talents.

While Danny saw many of his contemporaries make the move to Hollywood and flourish there, he was resigned to stay at home and become the poster boy for a particular brand of UK-made, independent movie.

One such contemporary who serves as a case in point is Jason Statham. Statham managed to make the transition from British films, such as Guy Ritchie's *Lock, Stock and Two Smoking Barrels*, to starring roles in Hollywood franchises like *The Expendables* with very little backlash. Like Danny, he had both chosen a lucrative niche for himself and featured in more than his fair share of mediocre action movies, but nevertheless maintains an untarnished reputation as a movie star and does not suffer the bad press Danny does. The key difference is Statham's keen protection of his private affairs and unwillingness to do interviews, limiting any possible public embarrassments and allowing the focus to be solely on his work. Danny realizes he might just be his own worst enemy in this respect, revealing to the *Guardian*, 'There are some actors out there that are brilliant at just acting and not giving interviews, mainly because they are boring as s**t and they've got absolutely nothing to talk about ... But if there's one thing I regret about my career it's that I didn't let my acting do the talking.'

Danny's constant presence across the tabloid gossip pages and his interviews on daytime TV shows such as *Loose Women*, *Lorraine* and *This Morning* were seen as good marketing opportunities, but only succeeded in cheapening the Danny Dyer brand. Fighting his natural instinct to swear or say something slightly risqué, Danny would end up tongue-tied, desperately trying to stay on the right side of 'family viewing'. While his 'take me or leave me' approach and unwillingness to censor himself is a refreshing change from the over-rehearsed responses of many in the public eye, Danny is often too candid about his opinions and his personal life and admitted to *Total Film*, 'Maybe it's time I pipe down for a little bit. I've lost out on lots of jobs because of my mouth.'

As if to prove this point, and acting as a counter-balance to the poor quality films and television documentaries he had made, Danny was continually encouraged to diversify and establish himself as more of a mainstream actor. He told the Female First website, 'I have started getting knocked by the critics and I'm not used to that, I'm used to people loving me and what I've done. They are saying that I'm doing a lot of the same stuff. I know it's just critics but I know that I haven't proved myself as an actor. I have maybe shown twenty per cent of what I can do.' Everyone working closely with Danny shared this view, supporting his belief that he had the talent to shine outside of the restrictive market in which he found himself. No doubt as an attempt to claw back some of his credibility and hard-earned self-respect, Danny's agents pushed him to audition for more period dramas and character roles, encouraging him to accept a greater number of interesting supporting roles rather than a few more lucrative, but ultimately less satisfying, leading parts.

Danny had tentatively expressed an interest in taking a role in a West End musical. *Oliver!* was a particular favourite of his from childhood, and he would audition for a part in Cameron Mackintosh's revival of the musical, which was set to open at The Palladium in London in January 2009.

Following the success of the BBC reality talent show *How Do You Solve a Problem Like Maria?* in finding a leading lady for the revival of *The Sound of Music*, Andrew Lloyd-Webber and Cameron Mackintosh were going down the same route to find a suitable actress to play the part of Nancy and revive *Oliver!* in London's West End. The other roles were being filled behind the scenes and Danny received a call saying the producers were interested in having him audition for the role of Bill Sikes. Danny was far from being a confident singer, but was relieved to see the Sikes role only required him to sing one solo song.

Danny's first audition went well and he got a call-back to sing and act in front of Mackintosh. Deciding he had nothing to lose, Danny embraced the opportunity, ignored the little voice inside his head telling him he couldn't sing and gave it his all. Danny nailed it. Although he hadn't actually been offered the role, he was confident he had done enough to secure it.

Shortly after the final meeting, Danny was invited to a party to drum up publicity for the launch of a new mobile phone. Keen to share one of the perks of being an actor with his family, he took Joanne along and after a few drinks, started to let his guard down. Talking to a girl who asked him what his next project was, Danny mentioned the Oliver! job and his dislike of the reality television method used to cast some of the roles. What Danny didn't know was that the girl was a reporter

Danny shares a close bond with his fans, and is always keen to meet them whenever possible. (**Above**) With authors and super-fans Jonathan Sothcott and James Mullinger for their book, *The Films of Danny Dyer*; (**middle**) smiling for the camera at a signing for his autobiography, *Straight Up*; (**right**) another fan takes a quick snap with her favourite actor.

Life's a stage: Some of the best work of Danny's career has come in the theatre, most notably in his collaborations with Harold Pinter. (**Left**) On stage with Nigel Lindsay in 2008's *The Homecoming*. (**Below**) The cast enjoys the after-party following *The Homecoming*'s press night, also attended by Harold Pinter (**seated, right**).

(**Above**) With the rest of the cast, (*l–r*) Neil Dudgeon, Anthony O'Donnell, Nigel Linsday, Kenneth Cranham and Danny.

(**Right**) Smells Like Teen Spirit: Danny with co-star Shaun Evans on stage for *Kurt and Sid*, 2009.

Family man: Danny took his whole family to the UK screening of *Straightheads* (**above**); with partner Joanne at the launch party for the Nokia 'Capsule 96' mobile phone (**left**).

(**Right**) Danny and his younger daughter, Sunnie, are clearly having fun at the Celebrity Soccer Six charity event at Chelsea's Stamford Bridge stadium.

Don't they grow up fast? Danny and Joanne take Sunnie and Joanne's goddaughter to the *Toy Story 3* premiere (**bottom left**); Danny with eldest daughter Dani, right, and a friend at the *Twilight: Eclipse* premiere in 2010 (**bottom right**).

All aboard! Danny's soap career sets off as he mingles with members of the *EastEnders* cast at the National Television Awards, 2014. (**Left**) Flanked by (*l-r*) Jessie Wallace and Shane Richie; (**below**) with his new on-screen family, (*l-r*) Kellie Bright, Sam Strike and Maddy Hill, as well as Wallace and Richie.

(**Above**) Danny stands with the rest of the Carters, including Danny-Boy Hatchard, far right, at the 2014 British Soap Awards.

(**Below**) Danny shows he is making a good impression on his fellow cast members as he has a laugh with Shane Richie.

East End boy: From London's East End to *EastEnders*, Danny's career has come a long way, but as head of the Carter family, a bright future awaits him.

and she was taping the conversation. His comments were reported in the *Daily Mail* the next day under the headline, 'The "new Bill Sikes" would do ANYTHING to avoid Lloyd-Webber's Nancys', where he was quoted as saying, 'I don't fancy any of those Nancys, they're all rubbish. It's more like, "I'll do anything to be on TV".' Needless to say, he instantly regretted the previous night's conversation and was not in the least surprised when his agent called to tell him the *Oliver!* production team had been in touch and delivered an abrupt rejection.

Danny was understandably devastated. The experience would have been a different kind of challenge for him, and could have opened countless doors in the West End, as well as provided a route back into television and film. It was also very well-paid, regular work, and the show eventually ran for over eighteen months.

It was situations like these that prompted Danny to hire a full-time PR manager to look over his press statements and help him tone down any potentially inflammatory comments he might make. Unfortunately for Danny, a PR manager is not on call all the time, and he still managed to let the odd clanger slip through the net. It was one such slip-up that scuppered one of the earlier approaches made by the *EastEnders* production team the following year.

Danny had gone to the BBC offices in 2009 to meet with their head of drama. When he asked why he had never been offered parts in any BBC literary adaptations or period dramas, the producers admitted his name did come up quite often at casting meetings, only to be dismissed because he was perceived as primarily a movie actor and would most likely turn down any small-screen roles. Danny, in an interview with *The Lady* magazine, expressed his frustrations at these types of situation: 'Sometimes your reputation precedes you, I suppose. That's not a choice of mine.'

Back at the BBC, conversation turned to *EastEnders* and the idea of Danny joining the cast for a limited time. They pitched a character intended to shake up the show, one where the writers would work closely with the actor intending to play him, ensuring the part would be tailor-made for Danny, and thus giving him a unique opportunity to have greater creative input in the construction of his own role. It was obviously a tempting offer. What Danny didn't expect was for the *Sun* the very next day to run a report stating he was in talks to join the soap, guaranteeing that a feeding-frenzy of speculation ensued. The massive intrusion into his family's private lives, which went hand in hand with joining a hugely popular flagship television show, was understandably daunting. Initially, he was diplomatic about the idea of joining the series, but as press interest escalated and the question of joining *EastEnders* kept coming up, Danny began to feel hounded and his responses became a lot less tactful. In the end, he was widely reported as having said he would consider it when he was 'fat, bald and fifty'. Obviously, this didn't go down well with his agent or the BBC, and the offer quickly disappeared.

Danny has spoken honestly about the downside of fame and often stated he has wrestled with its double-edged nature. Danny does, however, have a very vocal and forthcoming fan base and he never assumes the worst of anyone who approaches him in public – he will always stop and chat to fans, sign autographs and pose for pictures – after all, his fans are the ones who stood by him when critics and the industry itself had deserted him and he is keen to give them something back. He is well aware that this lack of privacy is the obvious price of celebrity and it is only when it comes to his family that he regrets he has become such an accessible piece of public property.

His attitude towards his fame and the success he's achieved is at odds with many people's perception of him. Far from being egotistical and self-centred, Danny has always displayed a deep desire to gain respect and acknowledgement for his work from his peers, and his drive to keep working is not fuelled necessarily by ego, but from a need to prove something to himself about his own abilities and to provide a secure future for his family. People's motives for working in an arena where celebrity and outside scrutiny are inevitable by-products are invariably complex and often contradictory – the actor who makes big-budget, commercial movies but complains about press intrusion and doesn't want to take part in promotion – but Danny accepts it as a necessary evil. He rarely directly blames the press or tabloids for any of his own mishaps or misdemeanours, more likely to say he only has himself to blame. He has spent more than his fair share of time in the headlines, for things he hasn't done as often as for things he has, but he never seems to let it get to him, and this attitude should be commended.

By this time, Danny was desperately trying to keep his career on track, but was fighting a losing battle to separate his public persona from the perception he was able to deliver a range of performances. For the next few years, he disappeared from mainstream films, seldom moving from within his comfort zone or challenging himself. With a steady stream of gangsters and hard-man roles and parts in several low-budget horror films, he was struggling to reach a wider audience. Sadly for Danny, his film career had reached a stalemate.

Danny retreated completely into the shadowy world of private investment projects and low-budget genre features. While working free from major studio interference, the world of independent film-making can be a breeding ground for innovators, but today it struggles to survive amid a climate of cutbacks and inadequate funding.

The process of raising the capital to make an independent film is often complicated. Money is the life-force for every venture and independent financers can be a ruthless breed who would see a made-for-DVD movie with a bankable star such as Danny as a sure-fire way to make a decent return on their investment. They are often given an executive producer credit on a film, and their desire to make a project profitable can extend from paying the actors a basic salary and rewriting scenes that seem too elaborate (and are therefore too expensive), to promoting the film in a misleading way via poster art or putting a famous actor, who might only appear in the film for five minutes, prominently on the sleeve designs of the DVD. Danny would fall victim to each of these ploys over the next few years, with the mis-selling of product to his fans becoming increasingly common practice.

The roles Danny was offered seemed to fall neatly into two distinct but very different categories. There were the low-budget British gangster films, where he might play a former villain trying to go straight or a regular man turned vigilante, invariably brandishing a gun on the poster or DVD cover artwork; or there were the even lower budget horror films that were a twist on the horror–comedy mash-up Danny had experienced on *Severance*. None of these were going to help Danny advance his career, and he was becoming increasingly downhearted and frustrated with the situation.

It became clear that Danny was guilty of underselling his own worth when choosing roles, saying yes to many projects that were not worthy of his talent and forgetting the financial boost his name could provide, part of the reason producers offered him these parts in the first place.

Around this time, Danny was approached for the lead role in a Sky television-produced adaptation of Martina Cole's best-selling crime novel, *The Take*. The story of a dangerous sociopath who builds his own criminal empire, only to watch it crumble and destroy the lives of everyone around him, felt like a perfect fit for Danny. It was a notch up from his recent output in terms of budget and production value, but he was ill-advised by those around him and turned it down. His team reasoned it was too much of a step back: he would be again playing on his old gangster persona and he should be starring in films rather than television miniseries. After Danny had pipped him at the post for *The Football Factory*, it was Tom Hardy's turn to get one over on Danny. Hardy made the character his own, picking up several award nominations, and it would be his last television role as he moved on to a string of blockbuster movies including *Inception*, *Tinker, Tailor, Soldier, Spy* and *The Dark Knight Rises*. While Danny has always been clear he makes his own career decisions, with his agents on hand to advise him, it would appear he was not being particularly well managed at this point.

Over the next couple of years, Danny became the go-to actor for low-budget British genre cinema, constantly working, but rarely making anything of quality and nothing which would survive outside the straight-to-DVD market.

By the time *City Rats* came along in 2008, Danny was desperate to be acting in something good, but was willing to settle for simply being good in something bad.

City Rats was a valiant, if misjudged, attempt by Danny to put a slightly different twist on a character he had played several times before – a young alcoholic with a violent past and connections to the criminal underworld – but one who strove to atone for his actions. Starring alongside his *The Business* co-star, Tamer Hassan, the film, set in London, contained interlocking stories involving a set of very different, but ultimately all fairly clichéd, characters. While aiming for *Pulp Fiction*'s story structure, the film fell flat on almost every level. The script was underdeveloped and amateurish, saddled with Hassan's obvious struggle to be a convincing leading man in what was a fairly challenging and dramatic role. The picture aims to shock, but ends up forced and unconvincing in its attempts to tackle controversial issues.

City Rats was a game-changer for Danny in the sense that it would become a major success on DVD, having been misrepresented as a gangster film reunion between Danny and Hassan. From then on, DVD distribution company Revolver became the 'home of Danny Dyer films' and insisted on packaging virtually every one of his DVDs in a variation of the same design. They would feature a grainy image of the actor, sometimes taken from a different film, with the standard black, white and red colour scheme that was now the pattern for gritty British gangster films. It would set a worrying precedent for the rest of Danny's film career and one that would become a major problem in terms of disappointing his most loyal fans. The issue wasn't restricted to his new films, as distributors picked up anything associated with Danny to repackage their existing catalogues and repromoted several older films in a similarly misleading fashion.

One of the worst cases of this was 2009's *Malice in Wonderland*. An ambitious but deeply flawed effort to subvert and modernize the classic *Alice in Wonderland* stories, it features Danny as a human version of the time-obsessed White Rabbit, transformed into a fast-talking, streetwise taxi driver who tries to help Maggie Grace's Alice with good advice and, more typically, some non-prescribed pharmaceutical guidance. Way too scary (and sweary) for kids and similarly too silly for adults, it's hard to see who the target audience was for this picture. In Danny's defence, it was a decent and slightly different role for him – acting as a Good Samaritan – that must have read well in its original script form. However, time and budget restrictions meant that getting the film-makers' original vision onto the screen was virtually impossible. A DVD cover with an image of bullet holes in glass (in the required red, black and white colours) gave no indication of the film's fairy-tale origins.

Dead Man Running was a simple race-against-time thriller, with Danny and Tamer Hassan playing a pair of lovable rogues using every dodgy contact and breaking every law in the book when they are given just twenty-four hours to pay off a debt they owe to an American loan shark, played by rapper 50 Cent. While this feels more like a true reteaming of the double act that had worked so well in Nick Love's *The Business*, the pair's chemistry was not enough to elevate the film's flimsy plot and overall amateurish execution.

Throughout the film, Danny looks tired, most likely due to the fact he was, more or less, shooting movie after movie over the period of a couple of years. Danny's way of working would see him map out a schedule of several films where he would play first or second lead, and then he would slot in as many cameos or appearance favours as possible in between. In the years 2008 to 2010, Danny was involved in making close to fifteen films, with nine projects released in 2009 alone. Towards the end of this prolific run, Danny was virtually on autopilot, and it's hard to differentiate the characters he plays in any of these movies. While finding a niche and playing to an established fan base can be very profitable, it's not something anyone hoping for the respect of their peers as a versatile actor would welcome.

For Danny, it was a trap, and although he admits he had a hand in making it, he was finding it hard to escape. Talking about being typecast to *The Lady* magazine, Danny explained the tightrope he was forced to walk: 'It's tricky. I have a job I love to do . . . Because of who I am or where I am from it has helped me get roles, but it has hindered me in some respects.' He remained optimistic, saying, 'You can't have it all your own way . . . As long as I keep working and it is good stuff and I feel like I can shine in it, then I am happy. But of course, I want to do period dramas and do things [out of my comfort zone] that make people go, "Wow". I am a serious actor and I am not just some cockney wideboy.' He concluded, 'There are some people out there who love me and really get me and there are some people who despise me and never give me the time of day without even meeting me.'

2009's *Jack Said* was a definite low point, as Danny found himself involved in a sequel to a film, *Jack Says*, that had made no money, but had a team of producers and a lead actor who were obviously desperate to make a name for themselves in the film industry. The fact that the producers were auctioning roles in the film to the highest bidders on eBay, and one of the lead actors in the film was a lottery winner who paid £20,000 to star in it, should have been a clue as to the depths to which he had sunk. By now, Danny had started to think, 'head down and get on with the job at hand', remembering there was a pay cheque at the end.

Danny was handed another source of easy income when he was asked to write a weekly column for *Zoo* magazine. *Zoo* had launched in 2006, riding the wave of other successful 'lads' mag' titles popular at the time. With their mix of football news, half-naked women and bawdy humour, the culture surrounding these magazines found its epitome in Danny. However, he saw it merely as a tool for free publicity, an easy way to promote his own films and personal appearances. His picture appeared at the top of the page and the content was largely light-hearted articles written in his 'cockney geezer' banter, some of which he supplied during weekly phone calls with staff writers at the magazine.

One particular issue, published in May 2010, included a reader's problems column, with Danny acting as the 'agony uncle' and supplying the solutions. Answering one reader's letter enquiring about what he should do after splitting with his girlfriend, the advice given was to '[Go] out on a rampage with the boys, getting on the booze and smashing anything that moves', adding, 'Of course, the other option is to cut your ex's face, and then no one will want her.' Understandably, there was a huge outcry as the story was picked up by the British press, and several domestic abuse charities, especially those dealing specifically with violence against women, took to every public forum available to condemn Danny's words and demand an apology. The *Guardian* quoted Ceri Goddard, a spokesperson for the Fawcett Society, the UK's leading organization campaigning for female equality, as saying, 'I can only assume that Dyer thought he was being ironic. But I would like him to explain that to a woman who is a victim of violence. I am worried that this does show an attitude that jokes about violence against women [being] fair game.'

Danny was soon trending on Twitter – for all the wrong reasons. It was an exceptionally tough time for him: hounded by the media, he tried desperately to tell his side of the story and set the record straight. Talking to the *Independent*, he said, 'Even as [the comment] came out of my mouth I wasn't proud of it ... But I never thought for a minute they'd stick it in the magazine.' He asserted he made the remark – actually a paraphrased quote from one of his films – as an off-the-record joke over the phone, and revealed he had never even met the journalists he spoke to at *Zoo*. Danny told the *Sun* newspaper, 'This is totally out of order, I am totally devastated', claiming, 'I have been completely misquoted. This is not the advice I would give any member of the public, I do not condone violence against women.' He continued to the *Independent*, 'It just makes me feel sick that people would believe that I'm a misogynist . . . especially with two daughters and having been brought up by women. I adore women . . . I love everything about them.' All over the internet, the story kept on going and nothing Danny did could stem the flow of negativity towards him. He spoke out repeatedly against being unjustly branded as a woman-hater and denied strenuously any suggestions he himself would ever consider violence against women as justifiable, but it was to no avail.

He was left high and dry by *Zoo*. The immediate reper-cussions saw Danny dropped from the magazine as they issued a statement contradicting his account of how the column had come to be printed, citing a production error rather than an editorial decision. He told the *Guardian* he thought *Zoo* were using the storm of bad publicity as a means to an end, taking advantage of the controversy as a way to drop him from the magazine. He speculated, 'Maybe they thought it was funny, or they were sick of paying me two grand a pop for a column I never wrote.' The damage caused to Danny's reputation was fairly catastrophic. Once a mainstay of daytime television chat shows, the fallout only served to push him further away from the mainstream audience he so desperately wanted to engage. It was a hard lesson to learn, but he remains philosophical about it, telling the *Independent*, 'I think the mistake I made was getting involved with a magazine like *Zoo* in the first place ... It's a publication that's about being [laddish] in the extreme. That's what they wanted from me ... I trusted them.' He then admitted, 'I sold out. I should never have got involved in it.'

He was forced to break cover to attend the premiere of his next film, *Just for the Record*, which was due to take place the same day the *Zoo* story broke. By merely showing up, Danny fed the media frenzy, and the press found any excuse to keep the story running. The film's opening box office was reported to be a minuscule figure, although it only received a limited cinema release in order both to publicize the DVD launch a few days later and to ensure it was eligible for video on demand. This had become common practice for the area of film-making in which Danny was now almost exclusively working. Unfortunately for him, the press became increasingly keen to report these ridiculously low box-office figures, neglecting to mention the real reasons for their poor performance.

The seemingly endless cycle of churning out budget features continued, and the latter part of 2010 saw the release of *The Last Seven* – a muddled supernatural thriller that was little more than a *28 Days Later* mimic, featuring Danny in a non-speaking role as the Angel of Death. This was followed by a string of low-budget sci-fi and horror films that included *Dead Cert*, *Devil's Playground* and *The Basement*. It is this last film that is seen by many as the nadir of Danny's career, so bad that he didn't even show up for the film's London premiere, instead drinking in a nearby pub with the film's producer.

Danny's professional life was at an all-time low. Stuart Heritage contributed a piece to the *Guardian* stating that, 'Danny Dyer has become the byword for low-budget, no-quality, Brit-trash cinema,' before adding, 'But beneath the cockney swagger there's a decent actor struggling to get out.'

Despite the odd critic noticing there was more to Danny than just an easy target for lazy journalism, for the first time in years, Danny was beginning to lose faith in his own abilities. He told Sothcott and Mullinger in *The Films of Danny Dyer*, 'I wasn't in the most confident of places and in my mind I had started doubting myself ... I started to think that I was a bit of a joke to people.' He finished, 'I was getting just, hate, hate, hate and I wasn't used to it.'

During this period of lamentable releases, a long-running battle of words with film critic Mark Kermode began, prompted by Kermode's continually scathing approach to Danny's work. While Danny has said he doesn't mind people having a little laugh at his expense, he felt Kermode's attacks were somehow more personal. The actor told *Empire* magazine, 'I know he's got to earn a crust of bread just like everyone else does, but he's got a serious f*****g problem with me.' In another interview with the *Independent*, Danny said, '[Kermode] thinks I'm the most ridiculous human being on this planet and that I shouldn't be an actor . . . I'm all up for the banter, but this is about feeding my kids at the end of the day.' He concluded in his autobiography that the criticism was more related to class and education than his talent. 'Clearly, he thinks I talk funny ... Well, that's how cockneys talk. Posh people think they're so superior to the working class.' While many assume every actor is immune to criticism, Danny admitted in the same interview with the *Independent*, 'Of course it upsets me ... Kermode thinks I'm some two-bob actor who does two-bob films for no money, who walks about with a swagger. When actually I'm a serious f*****g actor.' He believes Kermode is not alone in his underestimation and misunderstanding of him, admitting, 'I think I'm to blame for that' – a reference, presumably, to the lack of quality in his recent output.

Danny was making good money, but in real terms his film career had become little more than a treadmill of substandard material. When he did enjoy making a certain film or felt he had given a decent performance, critics were unduly savage. Even his status as a sure thing in the straight-to-DVD market was beginning to slide, as distribution company Revolver slipped into financial meltdown. After a particularly busy couple of years, DVD trade paper *Screen International* wrote, 'Audiences may well be suffering from Danny Dyer fatigue after a surfeit of similar low-life wallows featuring this actor.'

It was perhaps this 'fatigue' that caused a couple of Danny's better films, 2011's *Age of Heroes* and 2012's *Deviation*, to fail in such spectacular fashion.

Age of Heroes saw Danny teamed with his old *Outlaw* co-star Sean Bean in a story based on an incident from the life of Bond author, Ian Fleming. It was a throwback to the all-action films of the 1970s, paying homage to the likes of *The Guns of Navarone* and *Where Eagles Dare*. A bigger budget and exotic locations – the film was shot in the Norwegian mountains – saw the film elevated above some of Danny's recent work, but the film failed to stop the rot as far as Danny's reputation was concerned. Danny told Sothcott and Mullinger, 'What a great film! I knew that it was a film my dad would have liked . . . but it didn't do the business it should have done and again I don't know why,' conceding, somewhat pessimistically, 'It's just the f*****g spiral . . .' The film was a sizeable hit on DVD, shifting a remarkable 23,000 copies in its first week, but this success was not reported in the mainstream press and few were willing to give Danny the break he needed to kick-start a much-needed career revival.

It was a similar story for *Deviation*. Conceived as a low-budget film, it saw Danny play a psychopath who terrorizes a lone woman over the course of one night in London. Danny was excited by the script, telling the Female First website, 'I just thought that it was really brave film-making to just rely on two actors to keep the story going and keep it interesting with no gimmicks, there are no set pieces or stunts; it would make a really a good play.' Working with tiny, hand-held digital cameras during a series of gruelling night shoots, it was an intense but enjoyable experience. 'I just loved the idea of it because it is such a rare thing. I also wanted to get back to basics and get back to acting really, because it's what I love to do.'

On its completion, the film became the victim of distribution company Revolver's financial difficulties and was released during the same period as a mass exodus of most of its key personnel. This, along with the harm already done to Danny's reputation by his recent output and run-ins with the press, meant the film didn't have a chance. A particularly extreme review was written by Christopher Tookey in the *Daily Mail*. After a thorough assassination of much of Danny's work, he turned on the actor himself, asking, 'What's the explanation for Mr Dyer's consistently degrading roles, which serve only to show up his bewildering lack of talent?' The critic continued, '[He is] a very bad actor, with zero sense of social responsibility. Mr Dyer is very much a villain of our times. It's an illuminating comment on modern British film that he keeps being cast as a leading man.' Not even the most deluded optimist could spin that as 'any publicity is good publicity', and it sums up the opinion of Danny and his work in much of the British press at the time. It was the final nail in *Deviation*'s coffin, and subsequently, the film disappeared without trace.

Freerunner, again featuring Tamer Hassan, gave Danny his first chance to shoot in America. He admitted he took the job mostly for the experience of working in the States and the chance to take the family on a holiday while they were there. The film was nothing short of a disaster, with budget cuts during production altering virtually everything that had piqued Danny's interest in the script in the first place.

Danny was floundering. With money less of an issue after so much regular work, he started to take long periods off between jobs, and he confided to Female First, 'I sort of took a year out because I got a little lost and I was thinking about the pay cheque more than the actual film and I really need to stop doing that.' He noted, in an understated way, 'I know I lost a little bit of credibility along the way.'

An interesting change in direction for Danny saw him making a name for himself on post-watershed comedy quiz series. Multiple appearances on celebrity-baiting panel shows such as *Never Mind the Buzzcocks*, *Celebrity Juice* and *8 Out of 10 Cats* were probably intended as a means to mock Danny – the theory being that by giving him uncensored airtime and free rein to express his opinions on a wide range of subjects, it might result in him putting his foot in it and unwittingly create great comedy. These shows often used celebrities who might seem similarly down on their luck as easy targets for a laugh, but it's unlikely the teams behind these shows had any idea how wrong they were with Danny, who truly shone in this environment. Free of the pre-watershed restrictions that had previously made him tense and tongue-tied, he was genuinely funny, uninhibited and possessed an unexpected ability to laugh at his media persona. Turning the whole situation on its head, he soon had everyone laughing with him, rather than at him.

Several successful appearances led to Danny turning up as the most unlikely guest in Dictionary Corner on a special episode of *Countdown,* and eventually to a part in an ITV2 comedy set in ancient Rome entitled *Plebs*. Pitched as a cross between *The Inbetweeners* and *Blackadder*, Danny was cast as a gladiator in one episode and virtually stole the whole series with his hilariously deadpan performance (and a flash of his rear end!).

In February 2012, Danny took steps to make amends for his *EastEnders* slip-up a few years earlier, accepting a role in *Casualty*, and in so doing, getting his relationship with the BBC back on track. He realized appearing on such a high-profile and much-loved series was another important shift into the mainstream. Yahoo! Lifestyle reported him as saying, '*Casualty* is a massive show, so I was honoured that they asked me [to do it].' It was also a rare opportunity for Joanne and the kids to watch him in something relatively family friendly.

What was emerging was a newly confident Danny, aware of his developing comedic muscle and enjoying the chance to play around with his own public persona, often contradicting people's preconceived ideas about him with the varied roles he was willing to take, and showing himself to be a good sport, with a well-tuned sense of humour.

In this context, *Run for Your Wife* may have looked like the perfect vehicle to break the procession of low-budget horror and British gangster films he was churning out.

Beginning in 1983, Ray Cooney's adult comedy ran for nine years in London's West End. A huge hit, it became one of the most infamous examples of a uniquely British form of raunchy stage play – part *Carry On*, part farce. Cooney had spent the best part of thirty years dreaming of turning his play into a feature, and eventually, everything had come together and the film was scheduled to shoot the following year. Desperate for a change, Danny signed on to play John Smith, the bigamist taxi driver at the centre of the story who is desperately trying to keep his double life a secret from both his wives. Joining Danny in the other lead roles were Neil Morrissey, Denise van Outen and former Girls Aloud singer, Sarah Harding. Cooney pulled in every favour he was owed and rounded out the cast with a multitude of cameos from veteran British film, television and music legends, including Judi Dench, Cliff Richard, June Whitfield and Russ Abbot, as well as Bernard Cribbins and Richard Briers from the original stage production.

It's hard to imagine who thought it was a good idea to make the film at all – everything about it feels old-fashioned, and the innuendo-laden humour and slapstick are undoubtedly from another era. The end result was a bit of a mess: badly written and poorly acted.

The reviews were some of the worst of Danny's career. Anthony Quinn in the *Independent* summed it up, calling it a 'catastrophe', before launching into a truly memorable put-down: 'Never in the field of light entertainment have so many actors sacrificed so much dignity in the cause of so few jokes.'

The film's very limited cinema release generated a pitiful box office that became a story in its own right. Danny told BBC Newsbeat, 'All those cinemas were rammed when it was shown. It took £700 but the media don't want to tell you that story. They want you to believe it was in 300 cinemas across the country.' He appreciated he has become the easiest of targets, asking, 'Who gets the flak? Me, chuck mud at me [and] it seems to stick.' Gerard Gilbert, writing in the *Independent*, put it best as he recognized how much Danny had become a media punch-bag: 'The failure of *Run for Your Wife* was just the latest stick with which his detractors chose to gleefully beat the thirty-five-year-old cockney actor who once inspired our greatest playwright, but who now inspires such headlines as,

"Are there no depths to which Danny Dyer won't plummet?"'

Testament to the career slump Danny was in was the story he told on the film's red carpet at the premiere in February 2013, saying that he had been mistaken for a real taxi driver during the making of the film. 'People was like pulling me over and going, "Dan, I know your career's going through a bit of a bad stage, but are you driving a cab now?" It was a bit of a kick in the bum, to be honest.'

After the disaster of *Run for Your Wife*, Danny wanted to get back to what he does best and make a no-nonsense action movie. But this time he wanted to make something with a sizeable budget, high quality production values and a decent script. He was tired of letting his ever-loyal fans down and he was determined to give them a film he was proud to be in.

Ironically, *Vendetta* would also see his debut as an out-and-out hard man. It was as if Danny was giving in to his harshest critics and somehow managing to stand defiant against them at the same time. Contrary to what most people assume, Danny has never really played a hard man in any of his movies – he is usually a working-class anti-hero, a normal person reacting to extreme or violent situations, sucked into an unfamiliar environment or someone looking to escape their criminal past.

Vendetta was conceived as a twist on the *Death Wish*-type vigilante thrillers of the seventies, where, instead of an ordinary man forced to seek his own brand of justice when his life is turned upside down by violence, a highly trained former SAS interrogation officer uses the skills he has been taught to avenge his parents' deaths at the hands of a gang of criminals. Danny loved the script, he told Total Film. 'It's the film I've been waiting for all my career. I'd been pretty depressed and lost my passion and obviously the phone wasn't ringing. Then this came along. It was almost like I was being reborn . . . I had an opportunity to really show people that I am a serious actor.'

Director Stephen Reynolds had wanted to work with Danny since he'd seen him in his first film, telling his wife, 'I'm going to work with that man one day.' His infectious enthusiasm seemed to lift Danny at yet another low point in his life, reigniting his passion for acting and kick-starting his self-belief again. He said in *The Films of Danny Dyer*, 'He f*****g found me at a point in my life and my career where both fingers were crossed going to move on to the next level. He's given me this great opportunity and [the chance to go] back to *Human Traffic* . . . [he's] completely given me a lifeline . . . it has all come full circle.'

He was extremely excited by the potential to atone for much of his output over the last few years. He channelled all his pent-up frustrations about his career, his critics and the film industry in general into the part, and delivered a mesmerizing and authentic portrayal of a man deeply affected by what he's seen in combat. Driven by grief at the deaths of his parents, he also shows a gritty and unwavering resolve in his character's desire to make amends.

Danny was well aware he might be walking a thin line between condoning vigilante-style justice, but he argued, 'We're not saying it's right to go on that urban safari, we're just saying, "Would you, if someone you love was taken from you for no reason?" It's a powerful piece of work.'

The film's producer, Jonathan Sothcott, spoke about Danny in his book, *The Films of Danny Dyer*, saying, 'Although I consider Danny one of my close friends, the actor who came to work on *Vendetta* was different to the one I'd been on set with before.' He revealed that Danny was now 'determined, focused, an obsessive perfectionist. He took it incredibly seriously, and, of course, it shows in his performance.'

There is no denying the film is a massive step up in terms of quality – from the other acting talent involved to the production design – and Danny gives one of his best performances in years, certainly his most compelling work since his Nick Love collaborations. Everyone involved with the project came away from it feeling they had done their best work. Danny told Lovefilm.com, 'I'm over the moon with it ... personally as an actor, I feel that this has tested me more than anything I've done before.' He explained, 'I went to some really dark places on this film ... [and I] feel like I've really achieved something.' Sothcott added, 'What surprised me most about Danny, though, was how much he's matured, not just as an actor but as a film star – he has educated himself about how the business works, he understands the expectations his fan base have of him (and is very careful not to let them down).' He finished, 'There was a time when Danny Dyer the character and Danny Dyer the man were almost interchangeable. Those days are long gone.'

It would seem Danny had made peace with his past and was ready to look towards his future. The experience on *Vendetta* had settled his mind and he had determined where his career was headed. Danny was about to accept a role that would consume him, send him off into uncharted waters and change his whole life.

By the time it came to promote *Vendetta* in 2013, Danny was in quite a different place. A door that had seemed closed to him – in fact it had been more or less slammed shut a few years earlier – was about to be reopened. He had been approached again by the team behind *EastEnders*, and this time he'd said 'Yes'. Interviewed by *Total Film* magazine,

Deputy Editor Jamie Graham noted, 'Today is the fourth time *Total Film* has interviewed Dyer in the last four years, the first time he's made eye contact', speculating that Danny's improved demeanour, as well as his change of heart about joining the show, may have been largely down to him being 'in a better place mentally and a worse place professionally'. But Danny wanted to make it clear that, as far as he was concerned, it was a two-way street and *EastEnders* needed him as much as he needed *EastEnders*. He said to the magazine, 'The show's going through a strange stage and they asked me to come in to maybe give it an injection.'

While he would be the first to admit his film career was not where he wanted it to be, he was still working regularly. The real gain from the *EastEnders* job was diversification. He had much more to offer now and was determined to stop the rot that had set in over the last three or four years. He laid it out simply, 'I want to show people, a different audience, what I can do.'

It was this promise that excited the decision makers at the BBC. A new executive producer had been appointed at the *EastEnders* production offices, challenged with reversing the fortunes of the flagging soap, which had recently fallen dramatically below its expected viewing figures and slipped embarrassingly far behind ITV's rival soap, *Coronation Street*, in the ratings. With the appointment of Dominic Treadwell-Collins in July 2013, the message couldn't be clearer: the BBC was giving its flagship drama a makeover ahead of its fast-approaching thirtieth birthday.

First on Treadwell-Collins' agenda would be a complete overhaul of the story-writing process. Out went disaster-based plots involving fires, explosions and the untimely deaths of several cast members in increasingly far-fetched scenarios, and in came interesting, relatable and three-dimensional characters backed by intricate, slow-burn plotting and compelling storytelling. It was obvious that this would signal the introduction of some new faces to the cast and one man was key to Treadwell-Collins' vision for the future of *EastEnders*. That man was Danny Dyer.

CHAPTER TEN

HEADING EAST

When *EastEnders'* newly appointed executive producer, Dominic Treadwell-Collins, agreed to return to the show after a three-year absence, he already had a fairly good idea of what it needed to do to pull itself out of a rating slump. He told the *Radio Times*, 'When *EastEnders* is at its best, it changes the world a little bit. *EastEnders* isn't about propaganda, but it is about life, which makes it a very powerful show.' Away from the soap, as an interested outsider, he had watched as, in his eyes, his beloved *EastEnders* had lost much of that power, suffering an inexorable decline over the previous sixteen months.

Over the years, *EastEnders* had earned its place at the top of the weekly television ratings with an exciting mix of explosive storylines and authentic family drama, enjoying along the way its fair share of headline-grabbing press coverage. But by the start of 2013, things were starting to feel decidedly stale and the show was beginning to look more like a parody of itself than must-see TV. Newman's reign had been cut short when column inches, and more importantly, viewing figures, had started to decline. As David Brown commented in a *Radio Times* article in early 2014, 'Once upon a time, the show's tagline was "Everybody's talking about it". In 2013, nobody was, except to say how dull it had become.' Treadwell-Collins was determined to stop the rot, and his reign as showrunner would launch under the banner, 'Everything's about to change'. He had a plan. He was going to look back to the golden years of the soap – its 1980s and 1990s heyday – and bring back some of that old magic.

Treadwell-Collins recalled his early fascination with the show in the same interview with the *Radio Times*: 'I'd never felt an affinity with *Coronation Street* . . . I liked *EastEnders* because it felt dangerous, real and naughty, and also that it was saying something about life.' Part of the affinity Treadwell-Collins felt could have been geographic, he explained. 'I grew up in Radlett in Hertfordshire, which is about ten minutes down the road from where *EastEnders* is filmed in Elstree, and I'd go along to the studio and stick my head through the gates.' When the show began in 1985, Treadwell-Collins was only eight years-old, but undoubtedly he was as enthralled as the rest of the UK when the BBC launched its first primetime evening soap. The hype promised a unique mix of everyday family issues and a level of gritty realism that had long since evaporated from the cobbled streets of Weatherfield – *Coronation Street*'s fictional home.

EastEnders' first episode, broadcast on 19 February 1985, pulled in an audience of 17 million viewers, and within the space of two years the show had become a permanent fixture as the nation's favourite. The Christmas Day episode that aired in 1986 climaxed with the owners of the Queen Vic, Den and Angie Watts (as played by Leslie Grantham and Anita Dobson), finally ending their tempestuous marriage as Den handed Angie divorce papers. It attracted over 30 million viewers, becoming the top-rated episode of a soap in British television history – a record that still stands today. While never quite reaching these dizzy heights again, the show's characters soon became household names, evolving into some of British television's best-loved and most iconic creations.

Treadwell-Collins wasn't immune to the *EastEnders* fever sweeping the country, and it was his status as a die-hard fan and his general interest in how television was made that got him a job at various television production companies after graduating from university. He started in 2000, with a stint on ITV's popular crime series, *Midsomer Murders*, where, according to an interview with the Digital Spy website, he spent a year 'coming up with ways to kill people'. While that was a skill that would later prove invaluable in his role as a story editor at *EastEnders*, he would spend the next four years as the story producer on Channel Five's *Family Affairs*, which was sadly cancelled after securing its first wins at the British Soap Awards.

He first arrived at the *EastEnders* production office in 2005. When asked by Digital Spy what his dream job would be, he said, 'Do you know what? It's this,' referencing how his childhood fantasy of working at the nearby Elstree Studios was coming true.

Under his guidance, the show would refocus its original intention to deliver realistic, issue-led, family drama. It would strive to push boundaries in terms of tackling taboo subjects and his masterstroke would be turning the viewer's attention back onto one of the show's most popular families, the Mitchell clan, introducing the characters of Roxy and Ronnie and kick-starting a long gestating storyline that ended with the murder of the girl's father, Archie Mitchell, played by Larry Lamb. The show's most high-profile cliffhanger in years, 'Who Killed Archie?', would be Treadwell-Collins' crowning glory: A slow-brewing storyline that climaxed with the revelation of the killer during the show's first live episode, staged to coincide with *EastEnders*' twenty-fifth anniversary, in February 2010. That episode attracted more than 16 million viewers and acted as a respectable signing-off point for Treadwell-Collins, who moved on soon after. The offer to return to *EastEnders* as executive producer three years later, however, was just too tempting for him to resist and it signalled a massive overhaul of the BBC's flagship drama. He had seen the show at its best – even if it was as a schoolboy with his nosed pressed against the glass – and he knew what had made *EastEnders* essential viewing.

In an interview with the *Radio Times* in January 2014, he said, 'It's good to have one foot in the past while looking to the future . . . My idea is to make the show feel fresh with [the new characters], but also a bit nostalgic by bringing back characters we love.'

Treadwell-Collins unveiled his plan to not only repopulate the show with a few of its most popular characters, but also to bring back some of the best actors from the show's long and esteemed history. Over the next few months, his strategy saw Natalie Cassidy, Lacey Turner, Matt Di Angelo, Michael French and Samantha Womack returning to the Walford fold in the roles of Sonia Fowler, Stacey Branning, Deano Wicks, David Wicks and Ronnie Mitchell respectively. Treadwell-Collins also started a process of refocusing attention on the Square's main families; thus, Carol Jackson's cancer storyline would pull the Jackson clan back onto centre stage, while a heartbreaking plot involving Ian and his daughter Lucy would return the Beale family to the spotlight.

Rather than the overly dramatic, headline-grabbing storylines that had begun to plague all the soaps in recent years, he wanted to get back to what he thought made *EastEnders* special, the element at the core of any serial drama worth its salt: great characters. His dream of introducing a brand new family into the heart of the show would rely on them being believable, engaging and relatable. And he knew exactly who these characters should be – his own family.

Treadwell-Collins planned to base the figures of Mick and Linda – former childhood sweethearts and the couple at the head of the incoming Carter family – on his own parents. The Carters were a complete family unit of four – with various extended branches of the clan to be added at different points in the future – Mick, his wife Linda and their two grown-up kids, Nancy and Johnny, would move straight into the central, beating heart of the square, arriving as the new owners of the Queen Victoria pub. Treadwell-Collins was aware this technique had been successfully employed before by Tony Holland, one of the original creators of *EastEnders*, and he told the *Radio Times*, 'I always knew that [Tony] used his own family as inspiration for the Fowlers ... The Carters are influenced by my own mum and dad. In fact, Johnny is a bit like me.'

The family were set to be the most important new faces in Walford since the Slaters' arrival shook up Albert Square in 2000 with a string of dramatic storylines, including domestic abuse, secret pregnancies and convictions for prostitution. Key to his master plan was finding the right actor to play Mick Carter, and Treadwell-Collins had one man in mind.

Danny had been approached to join the *EastEnders* cast on a number of occasions previously, but either the timing didn't work or the part didn't interest him. When the producers made it known they were keen to sign him in 2009, he was on a film-making roll, having released nine movies that year. At the same time, intense early media speculation about his future involvement with the show made him nervous and he got a severe case of cold feet, said the wrong thing and consequently the idea was shelved. More recently, the roles being discussed just didn't feel right, as he told BBC News. 'At first I was, "No, No". I just wasn't really that interested ... it's always been the gangster or the villain and I thought, "Not really interested in that".' In an interview with Jonathan Ross on his TV chat show, Danny outlined his fears of being stereotyped: 'I thought it was gonna be the obvious: run about with a shotgun, have a tear-up with Phil, last about two weeks, get blown up in a car – end of!' He went on to reveal to the *EastEnders* Ultra website, 'They came to me a couple of times The last time was ... to be Carl [White]'. Danny went on to say, 'I'm so glad it wasn't the right time for me ... it was a good part, but there was no mileage in it.'

He wasn't wrong. Carl's character, eventually portrayed by Daniel Coonan, arrived in Walford in mid-2013, and was quickly revealed as bad news. He began a reign of terror that included blackmail, drug dealing and attempted murder. While conceived as a classic super-villain, Carl ended up as a fairly two-dimensional bad boy, becoming one of the first victims of Treadwell-Collins' wind of change sweeping through Albert Square upon his return to *EastEnders*. Coonan eventually left the soap in January 2014.

With Danny accepting Treadwell-Collins' offer of a part shortly after the latter retook the show's reins, it could be seen as the production team finally wearing him down. Maybe starring in a string of badly reviewed, straight-to-DVD movies had left him disillusioned about his film career and looking for an easy way out, but the truth was more complicated than just that. It's much more accurate to say that Danny and Treadwell-Collins were simply entering into a mutually beneficial agreement – they needed each other to progress their respective agendas.

Like the executive producer, Danny was a lifelong fan of the soap, telling Paul O'Grady on his show, 'I was brought up watching [it].' Yet he was also aware that things had not been going too well for it in recent times. But rather than proclaiming he was coming in as its saviour, he informed O'Grady modestly that he intended to do everything he could do to help return the lost magic to the programme. 'I think [with] *EastEnders*, when it's good, it's brilliant . . . [The show] needed a change and I was honoured to be asked to go in there.'

One of the contributing reasons to Danny's decision to join the series was the fact that Joanne was already expecting their third child. Danny knew this could be the perfect time to look for a more permanent source of income, one that meant he would be able to spend more time at home with his growing family. He was aware, however, that taking the *EastEnders* job would not necessarily be the easy option. Speaking to BBC Radio 1 shortly after the announcement of his joining the cast, Danny said, 'I thought long and hard about it and it's just come at the right time in my career. I've always respected soap actors because it's a tough gig.' He also joked with Jonathan Ross, 'I [thought] I should do something a bit pre-watershed for once in my life.'

More significantly, as he explained to BBC News, he had fallen under the spell of Treadwell-Collins' enthusiasm and obvious commitment to restoring *EastEnders*' former glory. He said, 'When I met Dom, within minutes I just fell in love with him. He's just got this amazing energy and when he explained to me the role, about taking over the Vic and coming in with a family, playing the alpha male, but not in an obvious way, it was like all my dreams come true.'

It was clear that Danny wanted a new challenge, and he was not afraid of the hard work he would have to put in to help the showrunner fully realize his vision for the introduction of the Carters and, in broader terms, for the long-term future of *EastEnders* as a whole. And it tied in perfectly with the developments in his personal life and recent career.

Treadwell-Collins would weed out several unpopular characters in order to make room for the new faces he needed to fulfil his ambition. Key to his strategy to reinvigorate the show was returning the focus to the dramas involving Walford's main families, and re-energizing its main hub, the Queen Victoria pub. The Carters were set to be the first set of brand new characters to go straight into the show as the landlords of Albert Square's main focal point. 'Stories are going to flow out of the Vic,' Treadwell-Collins told the BBC website. ' But it's not going to be the Carter Show ... It's going to be *EastEnders*.' He elaborated on this: 'This show works best when there's a bomb going off at the Vic and a bomb going off at the Beales' and a bomb going off at the Brannings. Not a literal bomb. I think that if you're stuck for stories you blow things up.' His agenda was clear: 'Let another soap win "Most Spectacular Scene". To be honest, I don't think soaps should be about blowing things up. I think they should be about character and people. And [they should] move you.' He finished, 'I don't cry about houses getting blown up.'

He reiterated his point to the *Radio Times*: 'EastEnders has got to shake up the audience. We don't want to do cover versions of greatest hits. *EastEnders* has to sing new songs, otherwise it doesn't feel fresh.' Stressing his focus would be on character over chaos, he said, 'It also has to be about people and feelings and emotions.'

Hardly radical, but it was nonetheless a risky strategy in

the television climate of bigger and better set-piece dramas, dramatic cliffhangers and controversial storylines, and Treadwell-Collins knew it would only pay off if he had the right actors. He also knew that casting Danny against type, as family man Mick Carter, would be his biggest gamble, but if he pulled it off, it would be the biggest coup the soap had scored in years.

'Stunt' casting and casting against type were hardly new ideas in 2013. Big-name actors have always been keen to appear in British soap operas – who could forget faces such as Sir Ian McKellen, Stephanie Beacham, Nigel Havers, Robin Askwith and even Peter Kay popping up at different times on *Coronation Street*, while *EastEnders* itself has pulled off some unlikely, but incredibly successful, casting choices. Barbara Windsor had ensured her place as a British national treasure through her work in ten *Carry On* films, but had never been considered a serious actress, when she first appeared as Peggy, the no-nonsense matriarch of the Mitchell clan, back in 1994. After a shaky start, she quickly found her feet, becoming a mainstay of the show for nearly twenty years. *EastEnders'* most famous, and arguably most successful, piece of left-field casting came in 1987, when comedian and all-round entertainer Mike Reid joined the cast as Frank Butcher. Reid enjoyed several extended periods in the show, turning Frank into one of the most fondly remembered characters in the soap's history. Reid gave Frank an unexpected depth, shifting effortlessly from the serious and dramatic to the comedic.

It was this kind of iconic character – immediately able to extract genuine affection from an audience – that Dominic Treadwell-Collins saw the potential for in Danny with Mick Carter. Tellingly, it was Frank Butcher's name that came up repeatedly during Danny's many interviews after it was announced he was joining the *EastEnders* cast. 'I loved everything about [Mike Reid],' Danny told the BBC News website. 'He was a real East Londoner, was so funny but had a real presence about him. When he was behind the bar, [you] believed it.' Danny asserted, 'I've got a bit of Butcher about me and want to bring a bit of Frank back.'

Like Frank, Mick Carter wasn't going to be a lone wolf; he would be a devoted family man who loved his wife and kids and would do anything to protect them. It was Danny's belief in Treadwell-Collins' vision of the character, a three-dimensional alpha male, but first and foremost a family man, which was key to his accepting the executive producer's offer to join the cast.

Crucially, this time he wouldn't be going in alone. The fact that some of the pressure and press scrutiny that he justifiably disliked would be diluted and shared by the other actors was a great comfort to Danny. In the same interview with BBC News, he commented, 'It's the right thing to come in with a family and not as a character on the periphery – it would be a lot harder coming in on your own.'

Playing Mick Carter would give the people who knew and liked his work a new perspective on him, provide his critics with something different to talk about and hopefully help him reach a whole new audience willing to accept his work at face value. Although sitting behind *Coronation Street* and *Emmerdale* in the ratings, *EastEnders* was still averaging 6 to 8 million viewers per episode, and joining the soap was going to push Danny into the limelight like never before: he would be reaching a massive new viewership, including middle-aged-and-up female viewers, as well as a youthful demographic – rather than his usual thirty-five-and-under male targets – who had probably never seen him in anything other than a tabloid newspaper headline. It was a perfect way to undo the misconceptions he had been saddled with after his recent film output. The opportunity to shake the general public's long-held perception of him, once and for all, was the cherry on the cake for Danny.

After only a few weeks on the job, Danny began to realize the scale and influence of the show, telling the *Radio Times*, 'It's quite daunting for us actors ... we've seen how much of an affect it has on the viewers. It reaches out to more people than politics, especially among the younger generation.'

Danny believes the only way any actor maintains credibility in a long-running role is to make sure you know who the character is, inside and out. By understanding what makes him or her tick and having confidence you can deliver as authentic a performance as possible, the viewer will be more likely to embrace the character and be invested enough to want to follow their journey. He told the BBC News website, 'The more you can make the character like yourself, the better – there's nowhere to hide in this game.' He appreciated he was being given the chance to show this new audience the real Danny Dyer – a devoted family man and loving father to his three kids. The awareness of the familiarity that comes with being thrust into the country's living rooms four or five nights a week, fifty-two weeks of the year, requires the actor to maintain a certain level of consistency and believability, he says. Danny concluded, 'It's about being real; you can't pretend.'

In an article published by the *Huffington Post*, Danny described the character of Mick as 'a nice guy', before elaborating that 'He's a normal guy who loves his family, he's a grafter, but there's definitely something there – you really don't want to cross him.' Reassuringly, this sounds like an element of the Danny we already know he can pull off.

Joining him in the first wave of Carters to enter the Square would be Kellie Bright, who would play Linda Carter, Mick's wife of over twenty years and the mother of his children, the couple's youngest son, nineteen-year-old Johnny, played by Sam Strike, and Maddy Hill as his older sister, Nancy. Not forgetting, of course, Lady Di, their pet British bulldog.

Bright has had just as long a career as Danny, although less high profile, starting as a child actor before taking roles in the the Ali G movie and the *Only Fools and Horses* spin-off, *Rock and Chips*. Strike and Hill, on the other hand, were relative unknowns, coming to the show with limited experience. Danny said to the *EastEnders* website, 'They're a complete revelation to people; they're a blank canvas.'

Mick would be introduced as the brother of long-time Albert Square resident, Shirley, and recent cast addition, Tina. The Carter clan would expand over the next few months with further additions, including Danny-Boy Hatchard as Mick and Linda's eldest son, Lee, Mick's dad, Stan, who would be played by veteran stage and screen actor Timothy West, and the family's Aunty Babe, played by Annette Badland.

The enormity of the gamble of introducing an entirely new extended family straight into the show's nerve centre, shifting the focus of the audience immediately towards the Carters, was not lost on Danny. He told BBC News, 'We're taking over the Vic – it's massive, you can't hide. It's an honour as it's the hub of the show.'

Success relied on Danny and his fellow actors establishing the new family's identity and back story very quickly. The existing link to an established character such as Shirley Carter was crucial, as was the viability of the Carters as a believable family unit. Each individual member of the group had to have his or her own distinct personality and flaws, Treadwell-Collins explained to the *Radio Times*. 'Soap operas go wrong when characters come in who all get along. We did a lot of work defining each member of that family, looking at how they rub each other up the wrong way, at the same time loving each other.'

Kellie Bright reaffirmed this in the same interview. 'There was a history already there ... it feels like the Carters have always been around and that's because there's been a lot to them from the get go.' Danny summed up his own feelings on the family's introduction by telling the *Radio Times*, 'You know, [Treadwell-Collins] really rolled the dice with us – there was a big build-up for the Carters and it could have gone either way.'

The question of whether the hype and Treadwell-Collins' gamble had paid off would be answered when Danny and the rest of the Carter clan made their first appearances in Albert Square over the 2013 Christmas period and New Year. Television critic Ellen E. Jones summed up the underlying problem facing *EastEnders* a mere fortnight before Danny and the Carters' arrival, saying in her *Independent* column, 'All good things must come to an end. Except for *EastEnders*, that is, which goes on and on, piling misery upon misery on Walford's residents.' She then proclaimed, with hopeful irony, 'How lucky for everyone, then, that a saviour is due to arrive on Christmas Day,' before concluding cheekily, 'Possibly, comparing Danny Dyer to the baby Jesus is a bit much, but you get the idea.' It would seem that, for some, the arrival of Danny and the rest of the Carters couldn't come fast enough.

CHAPTER ELEVEN

GET CARTER

Danny was scheduled to begin filming his first scenes as Mick Carter on the Elstree Studios set towards the end of October, but before then, he would have to face the full force of the British media and deal with the intense spotlight that comes with being linked to a role on *EastEnders*. On 1 October 2013, the BBC, after months of speculation, released a statement announcing that Danny Dyer would be joining the cast of their flagship soap, with his first episodes airing before the end of the year. Danny tweeted his followers with, 'Thank u for the love people it's overwhelming #eastendfamily. Finally my dreams have come true.'

The feedback was mixed, to say the least. These days, the reaction to any entertainment news and gossip is an instant burst of wild speculation and differing opinion across internet comment boards and social media sites, and it was much the same in this instance. Most saw the bigger picture and were willing to reserve judgement until Danny actually appeared on screen, accepting this was only the first step in bringing some must-see excitement back to *EastEnders*. TV critic Grace Dent used her Twitter account to announce that she was 'So happy right now', while TV presenter and 6 Music DJ Lauren Laverne proclaimed, 'Yes to this!' Consequently, the majority of media reports were fairly innocuous 'puff pieces', liberally quoting sections of the press release and maintaining a neutral stance as far as offering an view on Danny's acting abilities.

Ellen E. Jones, writing in the *Independent*, seemed to have a better understanding of Danny's true potential: 'There is a thin line between national treasure and national laughing stock and Danny Dyer walks it like an acrobat on a tightrope.' She continued, 'This might not be much of an asset in a British gangster film with pretensions to serious art, but in *EastEnders*, which works best when it's an overblown pantomime, Dyer has found his natural home.' Not entirely complimentary, but it appeared someone had grasped what Treadwell-Collins had in mind all along.

Despite the BBC stating explicitly in the press release that Mick Carter was a devoted family man, virtually every article or feature about Danny's casting began with a phrase like 'Hard Man Danny Dyer', 'Tough Guy Dyer' or 'Bad Boy Dyer', with the *Sun*'s front-page story headlined, 'New Dirty Den Is Dodgy Dan'. It was obvious Danny was going to face an uphill struggle to shake off the image most people had built of him over the years. But perhaps playing to Danny's perceived limitations was all part of Treadwell-Collins' master plan, and it was a bluff that would make the character's real persona all the more surprising.

Danny would be the first to admit he'd become typecast as a gangster or villain, but of late he had began to show a softer and more endearing side of himself on the more loosely scripted TV panel shows such as *8 Out of 10 Cats*, *Celebrity Juice* and *Sweat the Small Stuff*. Here, he was given the chance to show more of his own personality, a much more interesting, funnier and engaging side to a supposedly familiar character than anyone expected. Treadwell-Collins was banking on using the notoriety of Danny's bad-boy image – and the preconceptions of what that would bring to the character of Mick Carter – to pull in curious viewers.

While most people were unable – or unwilling – to separate the characters he played on screen from the man playing them, Danny has always maintained he never set out to be the hard man, telling the *Independent*, 'I've just done what's put in front of me. I'm from a council estate, I've never been media trained, I swear a lot, I walk with a bit of a swagger, I've played a few gangster roles, but I'm a sensitive soul. I'm a father to my babies.' He finished, 'I'm not a hard man. I can't be bothered with rolling about on the cobbles, mate. A mug's game.'

The real trick would be giving the considerably broader *EastEnders* audience a glimpse of this relatively under-exploited softer side, the side that Treadwell-Collins believed the public would fall in love with, the man behind the persona: the real Danny Dyer. The pair knew this would be the deal-breaker; no one would expect Danny not to be playing the villain, and this would hopefully ensure the viewers could relate more to Danny as Mick and, in turn, secure the unconditional acceptance of the rest of the Carter family, too.

As the media were discussing the new arrivals on Albert Square, another new face was about to make an appearance in the real world. Danny and Joanne's third baby arrived on 22 October, around the time Danny was due to start filming his first scenes at Elstree. The couple were obviously overjoyed about their new arrival, but Danny was especially thrilled – at last he had a little boy. He talked with wonder on Jonathan Ross's chat show about the latest addition to the family, who the couple had named Arty. 'He's such a beautiful little thing … I'm loving it. I was due a son, 'cause I've got two daughters, so I need a boy 'round me . . . I've got my boy now.' However excited the couple were about the new addition to the family, the stress of looking after a baby added to the anxiety and pressure Danny was already feeling about taking up his latest challenge.

He confided in an interview on the BBC News website, 'I will never advise anyone to go into a high-profile job and bang out a kid at the same time . . . It's been very hard.' He explained, 'I'm a hands-on dad. I'm trying to get involved as much as I can, but it's very surreal . . . You have a long, twelve-hour day, and you get a big chunk of dialogue that you gotta learn, but you're going home to a newborn child, which is not really ideal for resting and sleeping.' It was this increased workload that, although expected, still came as quite a shock to Danny's system. 'It's harder than I thought it was gonna be,' he revealed. 'I make films – a good day on a film is about seven or eight pages, that's a good twelve-hour day. On [*EastEnders*] you're doing forty-five pages a day, you're doing twenty before lunch.' He concluded, 'I like it, I'm ready for it, [but] it's really tough.'

Exhaustion aside, it was to become abundantly clear that Danny had made the right decision. He instantly felt at home in the Queen Vic and thrived on the bustling atmosphere of the set. He described the feeling of entering the studios to the BBC: 'When I first walked in here, it was, like I think [it is] for most people, it's a moment. It takes your breath away because [the image of Albert Square is] embedded in your psyche. We've grown up with it and then you are there and then it started to become real to me.' He told *Attitude* magazine, 'It's mad. I still can't get my head round it.'

When Danny described his first few days on the *EastEnders* set in the same BBC interview, he said, 'The fear was there. I couldn't help it. I've done a lot of work, you know, I've done plays at the National Theatre and I've done a play on Broadway and I've done high-profile things that are pretty petrifying, but this was up there.' Later, in an article by the *Huffington Post*, it was obvious this initial 'wide-eyed wonder' stage was wearing off fast, as the reality of the situation started to kick in. As a newcomer, Danny described his initial feelings of isolation: 'On my first day I queued up to get my lunch, but obviously I [didn't] know anyone, so I had to sit on my own.' He continued, 'A couple of them did come over out of pity, but it was horrible.'

The punishing schedule and unique demands of working for a show that airs four or five times a week were compounded by the fact Danny's entrance would be during the Christmas period. Historically, the Christmas Day episodes of soaps like *EastEnders* and *Coronation Street* compete to top the viewing ratings by unveiling a shocking twist in a long-running storyline, dramatically killing off a much-loved character or, as in this case, introducing an important new one. Danny told the BBC, 'I've come in at the maddest time – at Christmas … they're rinsing my character, as they should do. I've been in every scene. I've worked every Saturday since I've been here, it's been completely full-on.'

Added to the physical strain was the psychological challenge of processing the enormity of the role he was taking on. Mick Carter would be the new landlord of the Queen Vic, and would be joining a long list of some of the show's most iconic and popular characters. Danny was well aware that by stepping behind the bar at the pub, he was putting himself into the firing line. 'This is my stage, you know, it's my domain – this is the hub of the show. It's a very, very important role, and you gotta hit the ground running.'

He would also be filming the majority of his first scenes in front of most of the existing cast. Danny exclaimed, 'The first scenes I had were [at] Christmas [and] New Year, so you've got the whole cast in the pub. You don't know them, they don't know you and you gotta impress them, you know, prove yourself!'

But this was where Danny excelled. As he had done every time he'd been put in a similarly tough position before, he fed off the cast's energy and used the same competitiveness he'd always felt around other actors to deliver a series of strong performances. Danny explained, 'You gotta be on the ball in a soap. There's nowhere to hide. There's no excuses for not knowing your dialogue … There's nothing worse, I can imagine, then coming in here and not knowing your dialogue, 'cos you will crumble pretty soon.'

Any doubts Danny had about the acting credentials of his new colleagues or how hard they work were soon put to rest, he told Digital Spy. 'I've got a lot more respect for soap actors now. I don't care who you are – it's a massive test to be playing a character day in, day out with the amount of dialogue and the number of scenes you have to do every day.' He admitted he'd had a change of heart himself: 'I think there can be a snobbery towards soaps, and I'll hold my hands up and say that I probably would have been one of those people. When you make movies, you can sometimes look down on soap actors. Now I've got a newfound respect, just because it's really hard work.'

He revealed to *Attitude* that there were many new challenges even for someone with his long and varied career in the industry: 'The speed of it, you read the lines once, you shoot it. You've got to be on it.' He was using everything he'd learned over the years to fill out his character, who at this point was still an unknown quantity and set him apart, for now, from the other soap-opera actors. 'What I've tried my best to do is be very subtle. You can get into this whole thing in soaps with being a bit shouty and a bit dramatic, but for my character, I just want to bring it all back down.' He added with a grin, 'Save the shouting for your special occasions.'

As if to answer his own critics, who might have questioned his credentials as a serious actor, he told the *Radio Times*, 'If you're blagging it as an actor you'll be exposed once you come into a soap.' Danny confirmed the whole experience was a completely different discipline to acting in films; it was stretching him as an actor and he felt the need to instantly get under the skin of Mick Carter. He said to Digital Spy, 'It's very rewarding, but it engulfs your life completely. You're playing your character more than you have time to be yourself, which doesn't usually happen on movies.'

Danny also had to start modifying his infamously 'unfiltered' language. He told the BBC website, 'I gotta watch what I say . . . it is a struggle, I ain't gonna lie.' He explained that, as far as swearing was concerned, it had become a part of what people expected of him: 'I totally get I'm on a family show . . . so you gotta act a bit more family f*****g friendly.'

It wouldn't be long before the punishing work schedule started to take its toll on Danny, and although he had readied himself for it, nothing could have prepared him for the mental stress and physical demands of coping with his new job at the same time as having a new baby around the house. After just two months of filming, while appearing as a guest on topical quiz show, *The Big Fat Quiz of the Year*, he was asked by Jimmy Carr how filming for *EastEnders* was going. Danny replied in his typically frank manner, 'I'm f****d, to be honest. F*****g shattered.'

Shattered or not, Danny and his screen family – Kellie

Bright, Sam Strike and Maddy Hill – took a night off to attend the National Television Awards together on 22 January 2014, where they walked the red carpet to a rapturous reception. Any stress or fatigue they may have been feeling didn't show, as Danny and the rest of the Carters looked stunning on their first night out together in the public eye.

In just seven weeks, Danny had filmed nearly thirty episodes, and the media attention his character and new TV family had garnered had put *EastEnders* well and truly back on the map. And all this before a single second of their performance had been aired. After weeks of the BBC pushing the 'It's All About To Change' tagline in TV spots, magazine features and on billboards, Danny and the rest of the Carters were finally introduced in the closing moments of the show's Boxing Day episode, with the whole family instantly thrust front and centre in some of the shows most talked-about scenes in years.

After a teasing glimpse of Danny in an episode just before Christmas, the identity of the Queen Vic's mystery buyer is finally revealed as its former owner, the Square's resident bully and self-proclaimed 'Top Dog', Phil Mitchell, tries to clear the pub for the new owner's arrival. As he attempts to strong-arm his vengeful ex-girlfriend, Shirley Carter, out of the door, Danny comes to her aid, asking, 'Is there a problem?' Phil replies, 'I'm just chucking out the rubbish.' A more forceful Danny says, 'I wasn't talking to you,' and as Shirley moves to stand by his side, she introduces the stranger, 'Phil, meet Mick – my brother!'

Within seconds of his arrival, Danny had staked his claim as the new Sheriff of Walford. He had challenged a key figure on the Square and instantly ruffled a few feathers. As introductions go, it was pretty spectacular. The *Sun* reported,

'There was none of the coarse language or cocky bravado he has become infamous for as he made his small screen debut.' It added, noting the new arrival's impact, 'Danny was still trending twelve hours after the credits stopped rolling.' *GQ* magazine's website picked up on the nation's new favourite conversation piece, asking, 'Did you have a good Dyermas?', a nod to critic Grace Dent's 'Dyermas' hash tag, created well in anticipation of Danny's first appearance at Christmas, which continued to trend on Twitter for several days. *GQ* went on to say, 'There was only one place to be [over the Christmas period] . . . and it wasn't Downton Abbey. Albert Square had a new landlord for the Queen Vic and the excitement in living rooms around the country was palpable.'

As 'Dyermas' moved into Boxing Day, it was rechristened 'Dyer Day', and Dent herself would describe Danny's *EastEnders* entrance in her *Guardian* column as, 'a veritable coup', before singing his praises: 'I'd rather be stuck in a lift with [Danny] effing and blinding, than with the likes of Benedict Cumberbatch and his ilk who believe the art of chuntering scripts out loud in funny hats and prop department wigs makes them a messianic presence.' Perhaps a little harsh on Mr Cumberbatch, but there was no getting away from the fact Danny was finally finding some fairly outspoken supporters within the mainstream press. After a brief summary of the current ins and outs on Albert Square, Dent returns to her favourite subject. 'Did I mention Danny Dyer?'

Continuing the theme, Filipa Jodelka, in her *Guardian* World of Lather column, stated, 'Watching *EastEnders* at the moment feels like being released from a twenty-stretch in grimy soap jail', noting, '[Someone has] gone and made it good all of a sudden.' Rejoicing in what this might mean, she proclaimed, '*EastEnders* will never stop being stupid, but maybe it can stop being insulting and stupid.'

Even Charlie Brooker, the ultra-harsh TV critic who had mercilessly trashed Danny in print and on several of his television appearances, was warming to his charms. Brooker had previously stated, 'Dyer's presence on a movie poster has become a handy visual signifier alerting cinema-goers to the potential substandard quality of the film, unless said cinema-goer is so insanely enamoured with gangsters, football hooligans and rough diamonds who swear a lot, that they'll watch literally anything in which any of these elements feature.' But during his BBC2 show, *Weekly Wipe*, he re-christened Danny's character as 'Git Carter', saying, 'The old soap osmosis kicked in and, before long, I was caring about what happened to the characters.' Soon he was forced to admit, 'Rather than watching *EastEnders* so I could laugh at Danny Dyer, I was watching *EastEnders* because of Danny Dyer. He's a canny choice because there's something weirdly watchable about him.'

But not everyone was so positive. One tweeter worried Danny might struggle in a family friendly setting, saying, 'Danny Dyer without the bad language is like a tub of Quality Streets without the green triangles,' while another questioned his suitability considering his persona and some of his more widely publicized press stories: 'People have short memories when it comes to Danny Dyer. I won't be watching *EastEnders* with him in it. #gross.'

While the very nature of social media today means everyone's opinion is given equal weight, it would seem the balance was definitely on the positive side. Anyone who wasn't fully supportive of Danny was at least curious as to where his story was headed and, suddenly, *EastEnders* seemed to be talked about again – the hype had translated into something concrete.

The Carters were up and running. Dropped directly into the heart of the show, the family were set to remain the main storyline focus for the next three or four weeks. Mick and Linda were soon established as a loving couple, ferociously loyal and dedicated to their children. The strength of the pair was best illustrated by a scene early in the first few scenes of their arrival. Amid the chaos of the Carters' first day as owners of the Queen Vic, Linda turns to Mick and says, 'A new start you said, a new adventure,' to which Mick replies, 'As long as I've got you and you've got me, we can do anything.'

Establishing Mick's character as an individual was equally well handled, with some very deft writing. It wasn't long before viewers saw that Mick wasn't afraid to rub people up the wrong way to protect what was his and shield those he held closest. Danny's insistence that Mick was 'in touch with his feminine side' was neatly demonstrated when, in the opening shots of what was only his second full episode, Mick is seen preparing the family breakfast while wearing Linda's pink dressing gown – a running gag that was to feature in several more episodes to come. This was an image that was hard to reconcile with the star of movies such as *Outlaw* and *Vendetta*, and served to demonstrate that the soap's new star wasn't as one-dimensional as many had believed.

Mick Carter's character was, if nothing else, a refreshing change of pace for Danny, and his down-to-earth, no-nonsense approach to the part was swiftly winning him the sort of acclaim that had long since been absent from his film work. In Mick Carter, he had been handed a solid, well-rounded role and given some meaty scripts from the start, yet everyone involved in bringing him into the *EastEnders* fold knew the magic ingredient was Danny Dyer himself.

But the actor refused to take all the credit himself. He

wanted to make it clear that his decision to join *EastEnders* in the first place had been as a direct response to the enthusiasm and reassurance of Dominic Treadwell-Collins. Danny made it known he had every confidence in Treadwell-Collins, believing the executive producer understood what he was capable of as an actor and only wanted to make the most of his abilities. He insisted any initial doubts he'd had in his own mind about joining the show were put at ease by the assurance he would not be entering the Square alone. Danny was quick to remind everyone that his seamless introduction should be seen as a success for the whole of his new family unit, telling the *Radio Times* in no uncertain terms, 'I'm nothing without the rest of the Carter family.'

Summing up the experience of his first few months to Digital Spy, Danny said, 'I'm enjoying it a lot more than I thought I would. I thought I'd struggle a bit, but I'm absolutely loving working on *EastEnders*.'

Introducing all the Carters would take another few weeks, but with Mick and Linda quickly settled into the show, it wasn't long before their kids, Johnny (Sam Strike) and Nancy (Maddy Hill) were taking centre stage and making their own mark on Albert Square. With the immediate Carter family now all living under the same roof, the real drama could begin.

As Mick prepares to open the doors of the Queen Vic for the very first time, he asks, 'Shall we put ourselves on the map?' before proclaiming, 'The age of the Carters is upon us.'

CHAPTER TWELVE

A FATHER AND SON STORY

I t was clear from the moment of their arrival in Walford that the Carter family were bringing with them more than their fair share of baggage, and every one of them had something to hide. However, nothing stays buried for long on the Square. Even the seemingly solid foundation of Mick and Linda's marriage had its secrets.

The Carters' next big storyline, and one of the key story elements that had helped seal Danny's decision to join *EastEnders* in the first place, would involve Mick and Linda's youngest son Johnny, played by Sam Strike. Danny told gay magazine, *Attitude*, '[Dominic Treadwell-Collins] said, "Listen, I want you to come in as a family man. I want you to be alpha male. He loves his missus. Loves his kids. You're not going to know you have a gay son, he's going to come out to you, you're going to embrace it."' It was a considerable subversion of the *EastEnders* norm, as well as a major shock as far as Danny's public image was concerned. Danny was delighted to be given the opportunity to prove himself to a wider audience, asserting that he was going to 'grab this with both hands', viewing it as a unique chance to 'go back to basics' and focus solely on the acting.

Johnny's character was introduced as a bit of a Jack the Lad, but it is quickly shown that this is merely a front. Johnny's opening storyline would see him finally accept his own suspicions about his sexuality and admit to himself that he is gay, before eventually plucking up the courage to come out to his parents.

The set-up for Johnny's storyline was underway early, with a few shared glances with Gary Lucy's Danny Pennant – a character who had been noted as bisexual in previous episodes. This was all Johnny needed to make a move. After a few drinks for Dutch courage, and ignoring the warning he'd been given about Pennant – 'He'd flirt with a lamp post' – Johnny gives in to his curiosity and the pair end up kissing in the Square. When confronted by the few members of his family who do know his secret, Johnny states categorically that he fears that his parents, especially his father, would not be able to accept it.

As the story played out and Johnny was eventually 'outed' in front of his parents by his sister Nancy during a family argument, the scene was set for some revelatory acting that would go a long way towards changing everyone's preconceived ideas about Danny as an actor, as well as forcing many of his harshest critics to reassess their long-held prejudices against him as a person.

The whole thread is a masterclass in the unexpected, with an amazing script by veteran soap writer Daran Little, which challenges every snap judgement we might have made about the characters and teases out some extraordinary performances from all of the new actors.

Danny knew he had a fight on his hands if he was to successfully deliver a new spin on a familiar story. Key to this storyline working was Danny's ability to keep the audience believing his character's reactions, despite challenging their preconceptions of him as more of a one-dimensional bad boy. He told *Attitude*, 'Coming out stories have been done a thousand times before: The more typical way of dealing with it in a soap is that the hard man dad might have a problem.' Danny showed he understood completely what people might be expecting, though: '*EastEnders* don't usually do good dads. They're dysfunctional . . . The women are strong. The dads are s**t.'

Danny is especially strong in the opening scenes of the 'coming out' episode. The quiet stillness that Nick Love had praised him for in his early film performances is used to startling effect. It is obvious Mick suspects the truth about his son, but has made the decision to bide his time, realizing a soft approach is what's needed in such a delicate situation. Danny's key scene – the one that would soon come to completely define Mick's character within the show, as well as redefine the Danny Dyer brand that had become such a millstone around his neck – was an intimate two-hander between Mick and Johnny.

As the sequence opens, Mick begins by telling his son he can confide in him and he'll listen and accept anything he has to say, deflecting Johnny's attempts to use Whitney as a smokescreen, pushing him to open up about his true feelings. He says, 'I'll be honest with you, if I had a son who wore make-up and was all camp and that, I'd find it weird ... but I know that being gay is not a choice. It's just something in you. It's who you are.' He went on to tell Johnny gently, 'You can tell me anything, because you're my son and you mean the world to me.' It's an incredibly personal moment, and Danny's delivery is convincingly informal and protective. When Johnny eventually admits his sexuality, breaking down in his dad's arms, Danny's cries of, 'Stop it! I love you, boy. I love you,' are heartbreakingly real. As Johnny sobs and reveals his own disgust, saying he feels 'unnatural', Danny's reply is commanding. 'Don't you dare say that. There is nothing unnatural about you,' adding adamantly, 'As if you'd ever let me down. You will never understand how proud we are of you ... What you just told me takes a lot of courage.' Of course, it wouldn't be a Danny Dyer scene if it didn't end with a bit of banter. As the pair hug, Mick says, 'So you're the one we should have called Nancy.'

There was no aggression or shouting from 'hard man Danny Dyer' – instead, the episode ends with a shot of Linda listening outside the room, distraught and weeping uncontrollably. With rare subtlety and the volume turned down, there was very little in the way of the expected *EastEnders* trade-marked screaming matches and, by flipping everything the audience had been expecting to see, the story was given a refreshing, unique spin, and was all the more convincing and powerful for it.

Danny told *Attitude* magazine that he felt showing his son his full, unquestioning support was the natural thing for any father to do, adamantly stating, 'Why shouldn't they? If it was my son, that's how I would react.'

He had worked very hard to breathe life into Mick Carter and make him seem as close to a real person as possible, adding colour to the blueprint handed to him in early scripts. With a deep understanding of what was already there on the page and a fair amount of his own characteristic charm and humour, as well as incorporating many of his own beliefs and attitudes towards his own family, Danny had helped give birth to one of soap's most genuine father figures, and a rare example of a decent, strong, male character on British television.

This was a real personal triumph for Danny. He had shown a completely different side to his acting abilities, one he knew he was more than capable of, but which had only really been hinted at in his previous roles. He told *Attitude*, 'We did the scene three times; we nailed it. We got the right tone. It was perfect: just looking at each other in the eyes. There was a couple of times he dropped his head and I bring it up and say, "No, you look at me. You never feel guilty. I'm proud of you."'

Sam Strike, in the same interview, was also keen to praise the truthfulness of the writing in that particular episode, saying, 'That was really evident to me, in that it wasn't clichéd in the slightest. When the writing's good, it's easy to remember – it's what a human being would say, the natural string of words. It was what I can imagine the character would have said in the situation.' Strike also had high praise for his on-screen father, saying playing opposite Danny he had been forced to be 'completely vulnerable, completely open', admitting, 'The scene could have been a very different situation, where if I wasn't familiar with the actor playing my dad, I would have been a bit more reluctant, maybe not have committed as much.' He added, 'Danny's a really nice guy – very good at what he does. I just trust him. We both walked on set and were like, "Right, let's do this. Let's do it well."'

The immediate reaction to the storyline sent Twitter into meltdown, and the show, and Danny, were trending for some time after the episode had aired. TV critic (and self-confessed Danny Dyer fan) Grace Dent tweeted, 'reaching for the tissues again here', with many other viewers sharing her enthusiasm. One commented, 'That closing scene shows why #EastEnders is back in business. Tender, moving and artfully performed', while another said, 'At this rate #EastEnders will have to bring back the "Everyone's talking about it" tagline.'

Many praised the show for sending out a strong positive message, with one tweeting, 'A coming out scene on #EastEnders would never have played out like that even ten years ago. Nice to see times are changing. #progress.' Another wrote, 'I'm watching THAT #EastEnders scene from yesterday for the third time & it's still mind-blowingly beautiful. They should show it in schools.'

Some cited Danny's performance as being particularly noteworthy, one posting, 'Mick actually observes and thinks about other people's facial expressions. This makes him a soap first.' The *EastEnders* fansite, *EastEnders Ultra*, tweeted, 'OKAY! Do you love Mick Carter . . . OR do you love Mick Carter?! #BestSigningEver.' It continued, 'The new Carter family are marvellous! A new era for the show!'

Daran Little, the writer of the 'coming out' episode, also joined the Twitter discussion, thanking the fans for their support. 'Thank you all so much, really thrilled you enjoyed it ... really thrilled.' He then wrote, 'If you enjoyed tonight's #EastEnders keep watching ... it's going to get better and better over the next months thanks to @dominictc.'

The following day's newspapers picked up on the storyline, and the internet hype it had generated became a news story in itself. All of the positive feedback and free publicity was beyond the wildest dreams of everyone involved with making the show.

Paul Flynn posted an article on the *Guardian* website calling the scenes between Mick and Johnny 'exceptional', before branding Danny 'the daddy that every gay teenager might secretly wish for'. Joking aside, Flynn was keen to stress how simple and powerful the sequence was, rejoicing in the fact the show 'took [the gay issue] right into the heart of the family', and was trying to show a common, but unexplored, truth: 'that dads sometimes have an easier time of their children coming out than mums'. He stated, 'The scene achieved the holy grail of soap opera – it felt real.' Flynn's praise for Danny was unreserved, highlighting his casting as Mick Carter, and all the hype and expectation that came with hiring the Danny Dyer, meant that he was playing wonderfully against type, which in turn meant he had been 'gifted an atypically masculine soap superpower of being able to speak with his heart before his fist'. He ended, 'When Mick took his teenage son Johnny in his arms last week ... encouraging him to come out through both of their stifled tears, the hairs on the back of my neck stood upright.'

Audiences and critics alike were blown away by Danny's performance, and any lingering doubts about whether he had made the right move by joining the *EastEnders* cast must have evaporated instantly as Danny received the kind of glowing reviews he'd craved, but had largely been denied, for much of his twenty-year career.

Viewers were most definitely seeing the evolution of Danny as an actor first hand, and the character of Mick Carter was undoubtedly challenging many notions about not only Danny, but *EastEnders* and East End men in general. Despite having been exposed to some fairly extreme viewpoints during his childhood, Danny has never been shy about sharing his acceptance of gay people and their lifestyle, having always maintained an open mind and taken a fairly positive stance on the subject, even if, at times, it seems completely at odds with what many might expect from him.

Talking about his upbringing, he told *Attitude*, 'People are set [in] their ways really, and some were quite homophobic. It's never really what I was about. I was proud of my roots, because it's where my family is from, but I always saw the bigger picture. Going into acting and liking drama, I was [thought of] as being gay.' This was perhaps just one reason for his acceptance of gay people.

With any controversial storyline, there are bound to

be elements of the general public who will get upset, and Danny's core fan base was no exception. It became clear very quickly that some couldn't cope with Danny's involvement in a gay storyline, let alone such a sensitive and well-balanced portrayal of a gay man coming out to his family. A few of his, and the soap's, fans took to the internet to vent their outrage. Many were up in arms about the show's decision to even think about including a story tackling the subject, while others were simply disgusted by Danny's involvement.

Danny became an easy target for several homophobic comments via Twitter and Facebook in the hours immediately following transmission. One viewer tweeted, '#EastEnders was a disgrace. No wonder it was on after 9. Kids watch this program. Being gay is wrong and it shouldn't be promoted.' Another Danny fan said, 'Danny Dyer's son............ Is gay? Never cringed so much from *EastEnders*! That's not good. Poor Danny.' This was just the tip of the iceberg, and some of the comments were significantly more offensive.

Unsurprisingly, Danny was appalled by what he read. He told *Attitude* he was shocked at the response: '95% of the reaction was love, and people saying beautiful things and people saying "thank you" for doing it. But 5% was to the point of nasty.' In typical Danny style, his response was unapologetic and suitably blunt: 'Here's a little message for some of the homophobic pr*cks who are tweeting me........happy new year,' before he uploaded what looked like an ordinary medical text book diagram, but on closer inspection was a rather more interesting visual guide on where the homophobes could put their opinions on the subject. He joked with *Attitude*, 'I've had that picture for ages. And I thought, "I'll need that one day." And it was just perfect. The moment before I tweeted it, I thought, "Ooh, should I tweet it?" ... I thought, "Have that. Eat it."'" He went on, '[Then] I see it go insane, everyone backing me going, "well done." I just don't think those people should be allowed to get away with that.' The press immediately reacted to his reply, speculating it would land him in hot water with his new BBC bosses – a rumour Danny was quick to dispel. 'They backed me completely,' he said. 'I think it got 15,000 re-tweets. I gained, like, 100,000 [Twitter] followers that night.'

In the end, it was all good publicity for Danny and, more importantly in the BBC's eyes, for the show. The BBC's official statement, reported via the Mail Online, while not explicitly condoning Danny's response, was obviously supportive: 'The storyline has been largely positively received. Out of the 8 million viewers that tuned into the episode, we only received two complaints.'

Danny was getting particular praise for his sensitive handling of the story among the gay press and within the gay community – it goes without saying that his already substantial gay following increased exponentially overnight. He had for years enjoyed a sizeable fan base in the male gay community, as a portion of his earliest work featured gay elements, including his turn in *Borstal Boy* and on stage in Peter Gill's *Certain Young Men*. Nick Love's enduring fascination with the bonds formed between men – even if all the male characters are actually straight – also held an appeal for this audience.

Interest in Danny among the gay press increased during his run of Love-directed movies, particularly after the release of *The Business*. The images of Danny topless and in tight shorts turned him into a gay icon almost immediately, and in the summer of 2006 he gave a frank and revealing interview to *Attitude* magazine. The photo shoot accompanying the article was almost as revealing as the text. Danny discussed his own sexuality, asserting he was completely comfortable around gay people and, despite what people might think, had no problem with the lifestyle. Danny even hinted he'd had plenty of opportunities to engage with the same sex, teasing, 'I've had [my] moments . . . We'll leave it at that.' The photo shoot bore several images of a shirtless Danny, cheekily blowing smoke from his cigarette at the camera. One shot of him lying smoking naked in bed, barely covered by the sheets, would become one of the defining images of his career.

What might seem like a foolhardy decision to bare all, physically as well as verbally, proved to be a smart move, one which Danny was eager to defend in an interview with the *Independent*. 'I liked the idea, and I just got on with it. And actually it did me a lot of favours, especially with gay people, who assumed I was homophobic. They read the interview and saw that clearly I wasn't.'

Interviewed by Jonathan Ross on his chat show, Danny explained the importance of *EastEnders*' gay storyline among young men who related to his screen son and were going through similar situations. 'A lot of young gay men, who hadn't come out yet, they saw that scene and I was getting letters from these guys saying they came out the next day because of it – that's a powerful thing, you know . . . I was really proud to be associated with that.'

In the weeks and months following its airing, everyone involved in the *EastEnders* story received countless messages of support from youngsters who had found the courage to admit to themselves that they were gay, tackling their need to talk about their fears and worries about their own situation. Many stated it was thanks to the amazing work Danny, Sam Strike and the *EastEnders* writing and production staff had put into the storyline that they had made positive steps towards coming out themselves. Talking about the response, Strike told *Attitude*, 'It helped people to find a voice to come out to their parent and come out to their friends, which is the best response you can hope for because you feel like you've actually genuinely helped someone.'

In the same interview, Danny stated that, even months later, he was still a little overwhelmed by the reaction. 'I'm getting wave after wave of it. They're saying that immediately after the show they came out and it was the most liberating thing.' Danny was touched by the courage of his new fans and genuinely moved he'd given them the confidence to act, revealing that this was definitely a unique response to his work: 'I've had people come up to me after *Human Traffic* in clubs and go, "I took my first E because of you" or, "I head butted someone because I watched *Football Factory*." I've never had anything like that – really heartfelt.'

Talking to Digital Spy, Danny looked back at the impact of the story, keen to stress it had resonance outside of the gay audience, too: 'I'm very proud of the impact that Mick and Johnny's scene had. It didn't just have an impact on the gay community, but people in general. I'm an actor playing a character, but because of my media persona, people might have assumed that I'm homophobic or that Mick would have reacted to Johnny coming out in a completely different way.'

On the show, as the story unfolded, it would be Linda Carter who would now steal some of the limelight, as her struggles to come to terms with her son's sexuality caused her to do an enormous amount of soul searching, and created plenty of friction upstairs at the Queen Vic. It was yet another credible and very genuine situation, with outstanding performances from both Danny and Kellie Bright. It added one more layer to the developing relationships in the Carter household, and showed more proof, if any were needed, that the Vic, as well as the future of *EastEnders* itself, was in safe hands.

Over the coming weeks, further branches of the Carter family tree would be revealed to the audience at home – Mick's Aunt Babe would turn up unexpectedly, the precursor to the arrival of Mick, Shirley and Tina's estranged father, Stan. Played by veteran British actor Timothy West, he was quickly revealed to be a sly manipulator and would soon become a destructive and domineering presence in all of their lives. Shirley's son, Deano, a popular returning character, would bring Matt Di Angelo back to Albert Square after an absence of four years, and Mick and Linda's eldest son, Lee, a soldier who had served in Afghanistan, would come home under mysterious circumstances.

It was clear there was going to be no rest for Danny and, in the ongoing world of the soap, there is very little opportunity to bask in the glory of one's achievements. His extraordinary journey was set to continue for some time to come.

In his *Guardian* article, Paul Flynn commented that the arrival of the Carter family and their subsequent introductory storylines had, despite the hype surrounding Danny's casting, been a masterstroke in their avoidance of typical soap excesses. He stated, 'In a soap landscape of hellfire and brimstone, of explosions, serial homicides, train, plane and car smashes, the Carter family had arrived on nothing more histrionic than a note of shared intimacy.'

The 'coming out' scenes between Danny and Sam Strike and the teamwork and love he shares with his screen wife, Kellie Bright, were proof the new owners of the Queen Vic were a force to be reckoned with. The strength of their bond as a couple, as well as their unflinching instinct to protect their children, set them apart from most of the other characters in the current cast and helped the show reignite its unfolding dramas elsewhere. It was this connection to the central characters, and the ability to relate to them on a very basic level, that was winning back a lot of disillusioned *EastEnders* followers and converting a good number of new fans for Danny.

CHAPTER THIRTEEN

SOAPY BUBBLE

While the Carters' introduction may not have turned *EastEnders* into the ratings juggernaut it once was, it undeniably stopped the rot and created a much more solid foundation on which to rebuild the series. By mid-January, ratings were up by a million on the previous six months, and over the next few weeks *EastEnders* started to compete for the number one spot with *Coronation Street* again, the shows frequently exchanging the poll position. Everyone at *EastEnders* HQ deemed the whole exercise 'mission accomplished'.

Danny had scenes in every episode for the first month after his arrival. It was an intense period of work for him, and a full-on start to his new job. As the shockwaves created by Johnny Carter's 'coming out' story slowly subsided, the writers used the lull to add layers to the newly introduced characters, revealing more of the Carter clan's back story. Mick was becoming a truly three-dimensional character as Danny hit his stride, and he was able to start introducing even more elements of his own natural charisma and humour into the role.

On his return to work after a well-deserved three-week break, the show's focus had shifted to the other major plotlines that needed to be tied up before the scriptwriters embarked on their next big task – the build-up to *EastEnders'* biggest storyline in years: who killed Lucy Beale?

This slight let-up in workload allowed Danny to take a bit of time out to promote the show, keep interest in the Carters simmering and introduce his new audience to the real Danny Dyer – possibly the first time his newly acquired *EastEnders* fan base would actually get a glimpse of the man behind his new character.

As previously mentioned, Danny signed up to appear as a guest on *The Jonathan Ross Show* at the beginning of February 2014. This would be Danny's first major television interview since joining the *EastEnders* cast and, while it was still in a post-watershed slot, it signified another major move into the mainstream for Danny. It was the perfect opportunity for Danny to address some of the issues haunting him from the past, rehabilitate his image and let people see there was more to him than the clichéd hard-man image he was starting to shake.

Eager to talk and quick to share his rekindled enthusiasm for acting, Danny was typically candid about balancing his new job with looking after a newborn, before touching on the increased scrutiny he now found himself under. He confessed to Ross, 'I didn't realize actually, I've had a bit of fame for a while but since I've been in *EastEnders* it's gone onto another level.'

The interview was characteristically light-hearted, with Ross gently mocking Danny's recent film output, saying, 'Some of them weren't the best movies ever made.' Danny responded with mock fury, saying, 'How f*****g dare you.' He noted, 'I remember one year I did eight films. I cannot remember one of them.' Ross was quick to reply with a wonderfully deadpan response, 'Unfortunately, I can.'

On the whole, the episode was another baby-step in the

revision of Danny's bad-boy image. This was, however, still a post-watershed chat show, and the real test would come the following month when Danny, along with his screen wife Kellie Bright, was invited to join Chris Evans and Fearne Cotton as guests on the BBC's early evening entertainment and current affairs programme, *The One Show*. We can only imagine the cold sweats in the production gallery as Danny went live, hoping he would maintain the show's family friendly tone.

Appearing relaxed, Danny became animated when the subject turned to *EastEnders* and his relationship with his on-screen family. Sam Strike and Maddy Hill were also in the studio audience, Danny revealing that the whole Carter family was heading out for dinner after the show wrapped. This is a striking illustration of the dramatic change from the Danny Dyer of old, where a TV chat show appearance might lead to a night at the casino, followed by a tabloid-baiting bender. Kellie Bright (figuratively and literally) kept a tight hold on Danny throughout the broadcast, and steered him away from saying anything too controversial, while the hosts joked that they had a mystery guest who would be able to keep Danny in check should he turn potty-mouthed. When the mysterious guest was revealed to be Miss Flynn, his first drama teacher from his schooldays, Danny was visibly moved and, hard as it seems to believe, struck virtually speechless. He hadn't seen her in over twenty years and looked a little shocked when she joined them on the sofa.

Danny, of course, was able to refrain from using any expletives, and there was no need for the apology that Evans and Cotton undoubtedly had ready and waiting on the autocue.

Back on the *EastEnders* set, although the workload was no longer quite as heavy as in his first few weeks, Danny was still finding it a considerable challenge. A second wave of Carters was about to hit the square, but what he didn't know was that the groundwork was being laid for the family's next big storyline, and for the time being the writers and production team decided to keep Danny well and truly in the dark about what they had in store for Mick.

The extended Carter family made their debuts in the spring of 2014. Mick's father Stan, as played by Timothy West, is forced to recuperate at the Queen Vic after a bad fall, bringing with him Mick and Linda's eldest son, Lee, supposedly on leave from serving as a soldier in Afghanistan. It is soon revealed Lee is absent without leave, deeply affected by what he has witnessed on the front line, and has no intention of returning to active duty.

Stan is revealed to be cold-hearted and Machiavellian, soon expressing his twisted views but nevertheless managing to worm his way into the affections of the younger members of the Carter household. Shirley's warnings about Stan being 'poison', and her prophesying that 'by the end of the week we'll all be at war', went unheeded.

Danny particularly enjoyed sparring with Timothy West. A true professional, Danny had nothing but admiration for the veteran actor, admitting he was awestruck by his ability to still deliver. He told Paul O'Grady on his daytime chat show, 'The mad thing about Tim West is he struggles with his dialogue, he's getting on, but the thing is – he nicks every scene.'

The ongoing mystery surrounding Mick, Shirley and Tina's childhood teases out some very dark and painful memories for Mick, as childhood traumas begin to resurface and questions surrounding his, and his sisters', time in care begin to have far-reaching consequences in the present. Seeds had been sown, and within a few weeks there would be another explosive revelation to rock the Carter household, but first, the show had to deal with the murder of Lucy Beale.

A surprisingly sinister TV and media campaign appeared everywhere in the spring of 2014, and made *EastEnders* the most talked-about show on British television once again, with producer Treadwell-Collins teasing that the investigation and eventual uncovering of the murderer would carry the show some way towards the thirtieth anniversary celebrations planned for 2015. While Danny's character Mick was not apparently central to the story, it appeared everyone in Albert Square was a potential suspect. Mick and Linda's eldest son Lee, as played by Danny-Boy Hatchard, had a brief sexual relationship with Lucy, and became embroiled in the initial investigations following the discovery of her body, before heading back to join his unit in Afghanistan.

So, while certain members of the Carter family would be more involved in the mystery than others, in reality, Lucy's death signalled the end of their first phase of major plot threads, and during this brief pause Danny had time to reflect on what had happened to him over the last six months. He could be justifiably proud of his achievements, and as the show geared up to launch its biggest storyline since the Carters' arrival, Danny was happy to take a back seat and settle into his new position as part of the *EastEnders* ensemble cast.

The next landmark moment, and perhaps the crowning glory for Danny's *EastEnders* journey so far, was the announcement of the 2014 British Soap Awards nominations on 28 April. Danny had nods in four different categories in total and was the sole representative of the *EastEnders* cast to make it through to the final shortlist of nominees for Best Actor. He told Digital Spy, 'I'm quite excited and slightly anxious about it,' adding, 'I think the anxiety comes from the fact that I've only been in *EastEnders* for six months, so to be nominated for Best Actor is slightly overwhelming.'

Danny's only disappointment was the fact that his fellow cast-mate, Adam Woodyatt, hadn't been specifically noted for his performance as Ian Beale. Taking to Twitter shortly after the announcement of the final nominees, he expressed his disbelief, saying, 'It's a travesty. I'm voting for ya anyway.' He elaborated on this point to Digital Spy: 'I also feel slightly guilty, because there are some really good actors in the show – especially Adam Woodyatt with some of the stuff that he's been delivering lately.' He continued, by way of explanation, 'I think his big episodes just aired a little bit too late in the season, but he definitely deserves an award over me and I'll be the first to admit that.' But in the end, Danny was nothing but grateful to be nominated, especially in a category voted for by the general public, stating, 'I'm proud to be representing *EastEnders*, though, so I'm excited about it.' He later said to Paul O'Grady, '[Being nominated is] an honour . . . I didn't expect it . . . thank you!'

Elsewhere, while Danny was obviously thrilled to be nominated in the 'Sexiest Male' category, he told O'Grady, 'It's an odd award. I'm not saying age is a bad thing, it's a beautiful thing . . . I've seen the kids I'm up against – they were born in the nineties, they've all got washboard stomachs ... It's a nice feeling. It's good for the ego.' In another chat, this time with the *Radio Times*, he joked, 'I'm pushing forty, I've got a beer belly and I'm growing a pair of moobs. To every pot-bellied man out there, there's hope for you all.'

More serious nominations were for the hotly contested 'Spectacular Scene of the Year' award, for Danny's work with Sam Strike on the show's 'coming out' story, and with Kellie Bright in the 'Best On-Screen Partnership' category. Danny told Digital Spy, 'Of course Best Actor would be nice – that would be an honour as it is voted for by the viewers, so I am thrilled that I have made the shortlist in such a small amount of time. But it would be nice to win "On-Screen Partnership", because I'm nothing without Kellie and she's been a real strength to me.'

Win or lose, Danny knew recognition of this type was all the proof he needed to confirm his initial doubts about joining *EastEnders* were unfounded, and that the hard work he'd put in once he stepped onto the show had been worth it.

In his interview on *The Paul O'Grady Show*, Danny mulled over the leap of faith everyone involved in his *EastEnders* journey had taken. 'It wasn't a guarantee. I'd just met Kellie, my wife, I'd just met my kids and we all got thrown in at the deep end – "Right, become a family, be realistic." It could have gone either way. It could have been a complete car crash. But there is a lot of love between us all. I love them all. I'm rooting for them. I love it!' Danny went on to say that the main pleasure, as well as the most testing element, of his new job was joining an established company of experienced and talented actors. He admitted, 'To be in front of people like that, it's inspiring. All you want as an actor is to be inspired and I'm inspired by the whole [*EastEnders*] family. I'm so proud of it.' When asked about his future on the show, he was quick to underline he felt fiercely loyal to it and was now a fully integrated part of the *EastEnders* cast, saying, 'It's healthy that there's this rivalry – between *Corrie* and "that farm lot" [*Emmerdale*] – but I want to be in the best soap. I don't want to be second best. I want to be in the best one.'

It would seem Danny did indeed have his eye on the long game – an extended stay in Walford and a commitment to Mick Carter, the Carter family and an unequivocal pledge to return *EastEnders* back to the top of the ratings. There was no doubt the work was keeping the notoriously unpredictable Danny fully engaged, with much of his enthusiasm probably arising from his prior knowledge of what was about to unfold in Walford.

The focus was about to swing dramatically back in the direction of the Carters, shining a spotlight on Mick and his relationship with his sister Shirley.

After a failed reconciliation between Shirley and her estranged son, Dean, an argument breaks out in the Queen Vic, and finally we get a glimpse of Mick Carter as the Danny Dyer we have come to expect. Delivering on the promise Danny made when entering the show – that Mick's darker side would only appear if his family were under attack – Mick takes a swing at Dean as punishment for insulting Shirley.

With her relationship with her son at an all-time low, Shirley starts drinking and only stops after a heart-to-heart with Phil Mitchell. Phil tells her she should make amends and tell Dean she is sorry. Still drunk, Shirley runs towards the pub, saying, 'I need to see my baby . . . I need to tell my baby I'm sorry.' Expecting Shirley to run into the arms of Dean, it comes as a bit of a shock when she finds Mick instead, and falls into his arms sobbing, 'I'm sorry.'

It was quite a twist. Shirley turned out to be Mick's mother, not his older sister, a fact made all the more powerful by the story not having been leaked to the press beforehand. In fact, it had only just been revealed to Danny!

The decision had been made early in this particular plot's conception to tell Linda Henry (Shirley) about the storyline, giving her a veto if she didn't feel it was suitable. When she agreed wholeheartedly, the production team made the unusual choice to also keep all the other actors out of the loop.

Leaving Danny in the dark about the shock revelation was another of Treadwell-Collins' masterstrokes. The actor told Digital Spy, 'I did not see it coming at all! It was a complete shock to me. Linda knew for three months before I did and she didn't tell me, because she was told not to tell anyone.' Reflecting on the scenes the pair had shared in the last couple of months, Danny started to put the pieces together: 'I now get why Linda had been playing our scenes in a certain way. She's known all along, so now I look back on our scenes and think, "Oh, so that's why you played it that way!"'

Danny recalled, on leaving Treadwell-Collins' office, 'When I found out, Linda didn't know that I'd been told, so I sent her a little text message saying, "Hope you're having a good evening, mum!" She rang me straight away afterwards so we could talk about it.'

It was another example of the showrunner's new approach. In an era of spoilers and up-front press reports discussing plot twists and actors joining and leaving the soaps, the decision had been made to keep some of the show's major plot points out of the headlines prior to transmission. Perhaps Treadwell-Collins remembers fondly a time before soap opera storylines made the national newspapers, and the internet buzzed with gossip and revelations; when viewers would be genuinely shocked by the unexpected developments in stories and their favourite characters' lives. It was a policy that would pay dividends over the next few months, with many unexpected arrivals, departures and disclosures involving the programme's key characters and stories.

When Shirley's revelatory episode eventually aired, Danny was quick to send a message to his fans via Twitter, saying, 'I wonder what my Lady Di is gonna make of this? thanx 4 the love I'm as freaked out as u.'

The actor had nothing but praise for the show's decision to keep the plot twist under wraps, appreciating the extra dimensions and incredible shock value it would give the scenes between Mick and Shirley. He singled out Linda Henry for her recent work, saying in the same Digital Spy interview, 'Mine and Linda's scenes are always a joy. There's always this underlying thing there between us. I'm always on the verge of tears when I'm acting with her, because there's just something there underneath that you can't quite put your finger on.' He explained to Paul O'Grady, 'When I work with [Linda], there's electricity between us. She's a brilliant actress. I buzz off it . . . I love her with all my heart.'

Discussing where the plot thread was going, Danny told Digital Spy, 'This is a massive revelation for the audience, but they've found out a long time before Mick will. I think it's a while off [until] Mick finds out.' With only Phil Mitchell and Stan Carter in on Shirley's secret, at the time of writing, there is still a long way to go before the truth is likely to come out.

As things started to get back to normal for the Carters after the revelation, Mick says, 'What I want is no more lies . . . promise me.' Unfortunately for Mick, you can't always get what you want, and the family still had plenty of secrets up their sleeves, and as everyone knows, no secret stays buried forever in Walford.

With the dust barely settled on that week's twist, it was time to find out who'd won 2014's British Soap Awards. The ceremony took place at the Hackney Empire in London on Saturday 24 May, and the *EastEnders* cast and crew were out in force. Pointing to her on-screen husband on the red carpet, Kellie Bright said, 'I'm excited for him. I hope he wins.' Danny, however, seemed unusually reserved and distracted throughout the ceremony. His demeanour probably had more to do with the stiff competition he was facing rather than him saving himself for the Sellebrity Soccer tournament at Norwich City Football Club the following day. Perhaps he had an inkling of how the event was going to play out, as he failed to win in any of the categories in which he was nominated. It was practically a clean sweep for *Coronation Street*'s Julie Hesmondhalgh and David Neilson, who between them picked up six awards for their performances as Hayley and Roy Cropper in Hayley's heartbreaking cancer and assisted suicide storyline. It wasn't a total washout for the Carter family, though, as Maddy Hill picked up the Best Newcomer award for her portrayal of Danny's screen daughter, Nancy.

Danny posted a message to his Twitter followers the next day, saying, 'Can't lie . . . bit gutted about the awards thing. Just want to thank everyone who voted for me. Massive love to every single one of ya.' In reality, it is unlikely Danny was genuinely too disappointed by the evening's results, as the ongoing Lucy Beale story and the events currently unfolding in the Carter household were bound to push *EastEnders* back to the top, making them obvious front-runners for next year's awards.

It is clear that the Carters are set to remain a focal point within the show, with the *EastEnders* scriptwriters eagerly thinking up new ways to tease out their secrets and torture them with deeply buried revelations from their past. Everyone involved in the first five months of the their reign could feel justifiably proud of their work – and none more so than Danny. The great British television audience are a canny lot. They can sense real chemistry and won't be fooled by stunt casting simply for the sake of it. Dramas like *EastEnders* and *Coronation Street* only survive and prosper if they can retain the interest and affection of the viewers. Explosions and deadly infernos have little emotional weight compared to the most profound moments between a loving father and his youngest son, a husband helping his terminally ill wife take her own life, or the heartbreak experienced by a father on hearing his daughter has been murdered. Lucy Beale's death, the Croppers' unwavering commitment to one another and the togetherness of the Carters during their continuing storylines appear to be ushering in a new age of soap drama. One where human stories, and the real-life consequences that flow from them, take centre stage and offer the audience characters they can believe in and root for.

As a group of relatable characters, portrayed by the talented actors chosen to bring then to life, the Carters are unstoppable. As Linda proclaimed to her son, Johnny, 'There ain't no can't in Carter.' With the flawless creation of Mick, a unique, engaging and fully-rounded figure, it would appear *EastEnders'* future was looking secure. Danny could take a breath, safe in the knowledge that the door to the Queen Vic would remain open, with a pint waiting for him on the bar, for as long as he, and his family, desire Walford as their home.

CHAPTER FOURTEEN

THE FUTURE

As a piece of positive PR, or as the first step in his ongoing career rehabilitation, Danny joining *EastEnders* seems to have delivered more than anyone could have hoped for. Looking back over his first six months on screen as Mick Carter, Danny confided, in an interview with Digital Spy, 'I think there were a lot of people who wanted to see me fail, because there was a lot of hype. There's a lot of haters out there for me.' However, he had to concede, 'I think coming into *EastEnders* was probably the best move I've ever made because it changed people's perceptions of me so much.'

Speaking to the *Radio Times* in May 2014, Danny talked about the massive impact the *EastEnders* job had on him as a man, as well as on his career. 'My life as an actor has turned around so much these past months … I went through a stage where I made some bad decisions and became a joke. Now people are saying I'm a good actor again.' Danny went on to make it very clear he was fully committed to *EastEnders* and intended to be playing Mick Carter for quite a while, echoing the comments he made when he first joined the show, saying, 'I'm here for the twenty [year] stretch. As long as they want me, I'll stay.'

While it looks likely Danny is set to remain a fixture in Albert Square for the foreseeable future, he may yet decide he still wants to explore other opportunities, and not abandon his fifteen-year-old film career. He told the *Sun* in April 2014, when asked then what his long-term career plans were, 'One hundred movies, that's my goal.' It was clear he still got a kick out of film-making on this grander scale, and that may be where his ultimate destiny lies.

Over the years, he has helped generate an estimated £18 million at the box office, and although he admitted to *Attitude* that he'd had his ups and downs – 'I had a lot of success – putting bums on seats, then it went a bit to s**t' – it seems making movies was still top of Danny's wish list. Talking to *Total Film* magazine, he confessed he was optimistic that his *EastEnders* bosses would respect his desire to continue working on other projects: 'They're flexible . . . They understand totally that I'm not just this unknown actor . . . Obviously I'm appreciative, but if a movie comes along and I give them a bit of notice, they'll write me out for a bit.' He elaborated on this in an interview with Paul O'Grady, joking he needed to stick with film, 'Just so I can swear … I need the release.'

Danny's commitment to *EastEnders* was borne out in another interview with *Attitude* magazine, where Danny confirmed he planned to stay on *EastEnders*. 'As long as *EastEnders* allow it, I can flit out, go and do a movie, come back to Mick Carter … But at the moment, Mick's in my heart and I want to see where we can go with it.'

A few film projects had been mooted. One he accepted was a British gangster thriller featuring Spandau Ballet's Kemp brothers – Martin and Gary – which would see the rock stars return to the big screen together for the first time in over twenty years. Starring alongside Danny, it would place them firmly back in the same territory as their most successful acting excursion, *The Krays*, back in 1991. The film was directed by J.K. Amalou, who had shot Danny's *Deviation* in 2012, and filmed under the title *Assassin* in September 2013. The film was completed, but has so far failed to materialize and currently has no official release date – possibly due to the Kemp brothers' continuing commitments to Spandau Ballet, rather than a comment on the film's quality.

During an interview with Hunger TV in 2010, when Danny had just turned thirty-three, he talked about his future in the film industry, admitting it was a tough profession in which to maintain the quality of your work and achieve any degree of longevity. 'I'm still young and learning every day. I love the idea of writing and directing something, and putting talented, up-and-coming people in it, giving them a shot.' He revealed his wish to repay a debt of gratitude he still felt to the drama teachers who had first encouraged him and to the Interchange programme, which gave him his first step into the industry. He especially wanted to help those who might be in the same under-privileged position he had been in, hoping to provide help to 'people who haven't done the drama school thing, who are raw'. Danny also expressed his desire to direct his daughter, Dani (then aged just fifteen), in his own film, maybe going some way towards reversing the fortunes of her father and help her pick up the first BAFTA with the name Dyer engraved on it.

While both of these dreams remain unfulfilled, he was helping Dani get her first taste of the acting bug. When questioned by Askmen.com if he wanted to see his own children take up acting, Danny said, 'I'd encourage it. There are a lot of bitter people out there who have jobs that they hate and the key to life for me is doing something you love doing.' He concluded, 'I'll support her in whatever she wants to do . . . as long as it isn't lap dancing!'

Dani already had an agent by her early teens, and, after appearing in a small supporting role alongside her dad in *Vendetta* in 2013, it was reported in early 2014 that she had landed her first role – in a British gangster film called *We Still Kill the Old Way*. Confusingly, Dani would be starring alongside her dad's on-screen son, Danny-Boy Hatchard. *OK!* magazine quoted the film's producer as saying he 'predicted a bright future for this rising star', adding she had 'natural flair for acting like her Dad'. While a bit of nepotism might have been involved – the producer was Jonathan Sothcott, a long-time collaborator and co-writer of *The Films of Danny Dyer* – he stressed Dani had been hired on her own merits: 'Having known Dani since she was a kid I have seen her grow into a remarkable young actress – she has a very natural, honest quality and really impressed us ... I have no doubt she has what it takes to follow in her father's footsteps and become a bona fide film star and I'm really excited to give her her first leading role.'

Danny promoted his daughter by congratulating her on Twitter, saying, 'Proud of ya baby girl', but he would be all too aware of what she was letting herself in for.

Danny still has plenty of other ambitions he would like to achieve. He revealed his dream job to *The Lady* magazine: 'The obvious one would be Bond. A nice cockney Bond.' While Daniel Craig might have something to say about it in the short term, there's no doubt that the very fact Danny has put his hat in the ring in public means his name will undoubtedly surface in the frenzied speculation following Craig's eventual retirement. More seriously, Danny confessed, 'I also want to play a detective ... [Someone] who does not play by the rules but gets the job done.'

In light of the heightened profile he now enjoys, thanks

to *EastEnders*, it's not difficult to imagine Danny branching out even further. There is nothing standing in the way of him fronting a hard-hitting, quality drama along the same lines as recent television successes *Happy Valley*, *Line of Duty* or *Broadchurch*, and it's no stretch to imagine Danny bringing to life a contemporary literary character such as Jackson Brodie, from Kate Atkinson's *Case Histories* series, or Ian Rankin's eponymous detective from the *Rebus* novels.

EastEnders could indeed act as the perfect springboard for Danny, signalling a second stage of his career as a more valued, respected actor, capable of more challenging and interesting roles. Several of Danny's contemporaries have made the enviable leap from movies to television and back again, with many finding success on successful American television series. There is now an established practice of the big US television networks engaging the services of some of the UK's leading acting talents, such as Hugh Laurie in his eight-year stint in *House*. Shows like HBO's *Game of Thrones*, which has a cast that is predominantly British, have given the careers of many UK actors an invaluable boost, while actors such as Damian Lewis, Kelly Macdonald and Stephen Moyer had varying degrees of success in the UK before landing long-running and critically acclaimed roles in US dramas *Homeland*, *Boardwalk Empire* and *True Blood* respectively. Two of Danny's former co-stars, Jonny Lee Miller and Andrew Lincoln, have mastered their American accents and are currently enjoying extremely successful stints in lead roles as Sherlock Holmes in CBS's *Elementary* and as Rick Grimes on FOX TV's *The Walking Dead*. Even Danny's old friend Tamer Hassan popped up for a cameo in the recent *24* reboot, *Live Another Day*.

Although he recognizes the opportunities and potential rewards afforded by a move to the US, the main problem for

Danny has always been the thought of uprooting his whole family from the UK. 'I think that America is where you wanna be, but I should have done it younger,' he told *Hunger TV*. 'I'll never write it off ... It's just whether I take the whole family and go for it or not.' He finished, 'I know I could do it. I've just got to get my head down and concentrate.'

Being a part of *EastEnders* may have gone a long way to restoring his damaged reputation and resetting the public's perception of him, but more importantly it has helped restore his love of acting, giving him a much clearer idea of his own abilities and value as a performer. Danny's strengths and weaknesses are best illustrated in his portrayal of Mick Carter – overflowing with confidence, with an easy, masculine charm that runs parallel to his own personality. '[Mick's] the closest character I've ever played to myself,' he confirmed to the *Radio Times*. It gives the false impression that Danny isn't actually acting at all in the role. His on-screen wife, Kellie Bright, commented on the comparison on *The One Show*: 'Mick was a bit of Frank Butcher, mixed with the best of Danny Dyer.'

But there is more to Danny's performance than even he might give himself credit for. There is a subtlety and an awareness of the other actors sharing his scenes that sets him apart. It may be that his appreciation of them is down to his stage experience, arguably the most important facet of his acting arsenal. Over the years, Danny has learnt how to be receptive in a mixed group of actors. He is competitive, but never aims to upstage or steal the limelight by tipping the delicate balance of a scene in his own direction.

True to his original intention on entering the show, Danny has maintained the Carters as a true ensemble, and their strength lies in that unity, fuelled by the actor's determination to make their on-screen bond genuine. Danny's enormous contribution to that is his selflessness and willingness to share credit for his success with the rest of the cast, and it is testament to his insistence that he has no real interest in anything other than getting in front of a camera and letting his acting do the talking.

Perhaps, with this in mind, *EastEnders* might just be enough of a challenge for him to satisfy any unfulfilled career ambitions. Dominic Treadwell-Collins had put a lot of faith in Danny, giving him a fairly unique position on British television. By allowing him to enter the show with star billing, to instantly take centre stage, and set to remain a major focal point in the long-term plans for the show's future, Danny was in an enviable position. 'Mick is a really great character to play,' he acknowledged to Digital Spy. He went on to explain how the *EastEnders* experience was not only satisfying his needs as an actor, but it was also having a hugely positive effect on his personal life. 'It's a case of trying to find that middle ground between having exciting material to work with, but also having a life outside of the show. I've got a newborn child at home . . . so I'm also going home and dealing with that. That's been pretty tough, but like I said, the material is great and I'm really buzzing off that at the moment.' An extended stay on Albert Square would of course go a long way towards the rehabilitation of his film career and public image that he had been crying out for, but, more importantly, it would have the added bonus of giving his home life a degree of stability sorely lacking during some of his wilder periods.

Asked whether he had left his wild past behind in an interview in the *Guardian*, specifically mentioning his well-publicized involvement with drugs, Danny said, 'Don't be ridiculous. It's not ideal, is it, taking drugs and going home to a newborn child? You have to find a point in your life where you're like,

"Time to grow up. Time to let some brain cells regenerate."' It was undeniable that the drama surrounding Danny's personal life has settled down since he'd joined *EastEnders*. The addition of his third child, Arty, into the Mas–Dyer household, as well as the regular hours and more structured schedule necessary for his new job, had undoubtedly aided the transition from wild party-man to a more domesticated sort.

With his home life being as it is, is it finally time for Danny and Joanne to tie the knot? Speaking to *The Lady* magazine about marriage, Danny said, 'I should do now really after twenty years. I was going to propose a little while ago but we had a big row and she said, "I will never marry you." And I was just on the verge of buying her a ring as well.' When asked if he thought his children wanted their parents to get married, he responded, 'They don't really know any different do they?' He then admitted, 'Yeah, it's something we will definitely have to do. I mean it's ridiculous … I think we will do it [backwards], in the fact that our kids will be grown up and then we will get married.' With Arty turning one in 2014, it might be a while before Joanne officially becomes Mrs Joanne Dyer.

Speaking in the early part of that year, Danny opened up to *Attitude* magazine about his current state of mind: 'I'm pushing forty now. I like saying it. I'm on the other side of thirty, I'm thirty-seven this year. I don't think it's a bad thing. It's my way of saying, I'm changing.' Danny had made several key adjustments in his life: at home he was considerably more settled, and he had long ago turned a corner as far as drugs and alcohol were concerned. His commitment to Joanne was stronger than ever and the addition of his first son, Arty, would not only break the all-female monopoly in the Mas–Dyer home, it would give Danny a brand-new perspective on being a father. Professionally, as part of the *EastEnders* family, he had reached a much wider audience than he could ever have imagined in the earlier stages of his career, and had received a previously unsurpassed level of acceptance and praise for his work. While Danny had entered a new phase in his life, his core values, and everything central to his success, had remained fundamentally unchanged.

Danny had entered the dog-eat-dog arena of high-profile celebrity – from the initial choice to pursue a career in acting all the way to eventually taking a job on the BBC's flagship show – with his eyes wide open. Over the years, he had fallen foul to many of the pitfalls littering the road to success. He consistently shunned the media intrusion that now seemed to go hand in hand with his industry, uncomfortable with the apparently inseparable association between celebrity and his chosen profession. Although he loved it, acting for Danny was a job, first and foremost – a view not always taken by certain sections of the industry, which simply appeared hungry for fame and the fleeting notoriety it could bring them. He was justifiably proud of his career achievements, of working hard for most of his adult life, and was more than willing to hold his hand up and admit where he'd gone wrong.

But Danny possessed a driving ambition, an unwavering enthusiasm and unlimited energy, which made him all the more determined to remain focused on the job at hand: developing as an actor and providing for his family. As his character, Frankie, in *The Business*, says, 'I'd rather be someone for a day than no one for a lifetime.'

Danny seems to have approached *EastEnders*, and his future in the acting profession, with the same fighting spirit he'd brought to every other challenge he'd experienced in his early years and throughout his career. He may have struggled and fought to overcome a difficult start in life, but he remains immensely proud of his humble London roots. Danny recognizes the fact that these early battles gave him the dogged determination to do things on his own terms and fuelled the drive and confidence he had to succeed, with little help from anyone outside of his close-knit family. The lack of an early helping-hand, in term of connections within the industry, only made his eventual success that much sweeter, justifying his decision to fiercely defend his status as an outsider, a champion of independent cinema and someone who tries to remain, often stubbornly and detrimentally, true to himself. Through his choice of a relatively understated family home, his loyalty to his beloved West Ham and the genuine nature of his portrayal of Mick Carter, Danny remains connected to the family, his friends and the places that shaped him – he remains a real East End boy.

SOURCES

NEWSPAPERS AND MAGAZINES

Attitude
Daily Mail
Daily Star
Empire
Evening Standard
Front
GQ
Guardian
Hollywood Reporter
Independent
The Lady
Loaded
Mail On Sunday
Mirror
The New York Times
NME
Nuts
Observer
OK!
Q
Radio Times
Rolling Stone
Screen International
Sun

Sunday Mirror
Sunday People
The Sunday Times
Telegraph
Total Film
Variety

ONLINE

Anewdirection.org.uk (A New Direction for Arts)
Askmen.com
BBC.co.uk/film
BBC.co.uk/news
BBC.co.uk/radio1
Cinema.com
Digitalspy.co.uk
Eastendersultra.co.uk
Empireonline.com
Facebook.com
Femalefirst.co.uk
Film4.com
Huffington Post
Hungertv.com
Lovefilm.com
Sickchirpse.com
Thesun.co.uk
Twitter.com
UK.lifestyle.yahoo.com

BOOKS

Dyer, Danny *Straight Up*, Arrow Books, 2010
Goldman, William *Adventures in the Screen Trade*, Abacus, 1996
Mullinger, James, Sothcott, Jonathan *The Films of Danny Dyer*, Caffeine Nights Publishing, 2013

FILMS AND TELEVISION

Borstal Boy
The Business
Charlie Brooker's Weekly Wipe
Deviation
The Football Factory
Goodbye Charlie Bright
Human Traffic
The Jonathan Ross Show
The Last Seven
Loose Women
Malice in Wonderland
Nothing To Something: Danny Dyer
The One Show
The Paul O'Grady Show
Prime Suspect 3
Run For Your Wife
Severance
Straightheads
The Trench
Vendetta

PICTURE ACKNOWLEDGEMENTS

Page 1: REX/ITV (both)

Page 2: Michael Crabtree/PA Images (top); REX/Moviestore Collection (bottom)

Page 3: REX/Moviestore Collection (top); Doug Peters/EMPICS/PA Images (bottom)

Page 4: Gareth Davies/Getty Images (top); Myung Jung Kim/PA Images (bottom)

Page 5: Rex/Snap Stills (both)

Page 6: © Photos 12/Alamy (top); Martial Trezzini/PA Images (bottom)

Page 7: REX/Moviestore Collection (top); Dave M. Benett/Getty Images (bottom)

Page 8: REX (top left); © Revolver/Everett/REX (top right); Beretta/Sims/REX (bottom)

Page 9: Joshua Lawrence/REX (top); Emma Coles/EMPICS/PA Images (middle); Max Nash/AFP/Getty Images (bottom)

Page 10: REX/Alastair Muir (top); Dave M Benett/Getty Images (bottom)

Page 11: © Geraint Lewis/Alamy (top); REX/Alastair Muir (bottom)

Page 12: Dave M. Benett/Getty Images (top); JAB Promotions/WireImage/Getty Images (bottom)

Page 13: Beretta/Sims/REX (top); REX/Rory Gilder (bottom left); Yui Mok/PA Images (bottom right)

Page 14: Dave J Hogan/Getty Images (both)

Page 15: Ian West/PA Wire/PA Images (top); Dave M. Benett/Getty Images (bottom)

Page 16: Dave M. Benett/Getty Images

INDEX

(The initials DD refer to Danny Dyer)

A New Direction for Arts (AND) 24
Abbot, Russ 145
Academy Awards 9, 95
Adulthood 121
Adventures in the Screen Trade
    (Goldman) 9
Afghan War 111
Age of Heroes 141
Ali G 162
Alice in Wonderland 134
All in the Game 120
All the President's Men 9
All Star Mr & Mrs 122
Allen, Keith 61–2, 80
Allen, Lily 122–3
Almeida Theatre 61, 62
Amalou, J.K. 203
Anderson, Gillian 7, 115–16, 120
Arnold, Andrea 94–5
Askmen.com 16, 36, 203
Askwith, Robin 159
Assassin 203
Atkinson, Kate 205
Atkinson, Rowan 72
Attitude 58, 167, 169, 176, 178, 179,
    180, 182, 183, 184–6, 202, 208

Backpacker's Guide to Thailand, The
    96–7
Badland, Annette 162
BAFTA Awards 30, 203
Basement, The 139
BBC 209
BBC Film 104
BBC News 8
BBC Three 122
Beacham, Stephanie 159

Beale, Ian 7
Bean, Sean 110, 111, 141
Behan, Brendan 52
    film representation of 53
Bend It Like Beckham 86
Berry, Halle 74
Big Fat Quiz of the Year, The 170
Bill, The 31
Billy Elliot 25
Blackadder 144
Blitz 15
Boardwalk Empire 205
Bolan, Marc 13
borstal 52, 53, 55
Borstal Boy (book) (Behan) 52
Borstal Boy (film) 52–5, 184
Boyd, William 46, 48, 49, 51
Boyle, Danny 28, 41, 42
Bradshaw, Peter 42
Bravo 109, 110, 124
Briers, Richard 145
Bright, Kellie 162, 163, 170, 186, 191,
    194–5, 198, 206
Brit-trash 140
British Soap Awards 153, 193–5, 198
Broadchurch 205
Broadway 168
Brooker, Charlie 173
Brown, David 151
Bryant, Det. Sammy (fictional) 53
Business, The 97, 98, 99–106, 109,
    134, 135, 184, 209
    authentic detail applied to 101–2
    Lads' mags' appreciation of 105

Cadfael 31, 32
Cage, Nicholas 74
Caine, Michael 125
Cannes Film Festival 98

Cannon, Danny 33
Capaldi, Peter 28
Carr, Jimmy 170
Carry On... 144, 159
Case Histories 205
Casino 105
Casino Royale 75
Cassidy, Natalie 154
Casualty 144
Celebration 57, 59–61, 62, 79
    New York run of 77–81
Celebrity Juice 143, 165
Certain Young Men 57–9, 184
Channel 4 94
Channel Five 153
Chapman, Georgina 103
Chemical Brothers 40
City Rats 133–4
Clarke, Noel 121
Clay, Thomas 97
Clockwork Orange, A 17
Closure 117
club culture 40–1
Cobain, Kurt 84
Cole, Martina 133
Coonan, Daniel 156
Cooney, Ray 144
Coronation Street 149, 152, 159, 160,
    168, 189, 195, 199
Costa del Crime 99
Costner, Kevin 53
Cotton, Fearne 22, 191
Countdown 144
Cracker 44
Craig, Daniel 47, 50, 75, 204
Creep 106
Cribbins, Bernard 145
CSI 33
Cumberbatch, Benedict 172
Custom House 14, 21

Daily Mail 129, 142
Daily Telegraph 125

Danny Dyer's Deadliest Men 109, 112,
    124
*Danny Dyer's Deadliest Men 2: Living
    Dangerously* 110, 112, 124, 125
D'Arcy, James 48
Dark Knight Rises, The 133
David, Craig 68
Day-Lewis, Daniel 9
Dead Cert 139
Dead Man Running 135
Death Wish 146
Dench, Judi 145
Dent, Grace 164, 172, 180
Deviation 141, 142, 203
Devil's Playground 139
Di Angelo, Matt 154, 187
Digital Spy 123, 153, 169, 170, 186,
    193, 194, 195, 197, 198, 201, 207
Dobson, Anita 152
Doctor Who 28
Dodger, Artful 68
domestic violence 137–8
Double Jeopardy 53
Duncan, Lindsay 61
Dyer, Antony (father) 28, 29, 46, 141
    infidelity of 16
Dyer, Arty (son) 157, 161, 207, 208
    birth of 166–7
Dyer, Christine (mother) 16, 18, 28,
    46, 104
    drama groups attended by 23
Dyer, Dani (daughter) 39, 64, 67, 70,
    75, 81, 85, 92, 93, 97, 104, 107,
    121, 166, 203
    acting career of 204
    birth of 37
    schooling of 124
Dyer, Danny:
    affairs of 70–1, 75, 77, 78, 79, 83,
        85, 92–3, 123
    agents of 26–7, 32, 56, 57, 86–7,
        118, 119, 129, 130
    as agony uncle 137

and alcohol 18, 19, 45, 56, 64, 68–
70, 71, 75, 80–1, 83, 84, 85, 86,
90, 106–7, 122
All Star Mr & Mrs appearance of
122
anger problems of 18, 37
Artful Dodger-like nature of 18
auditions undertaken by 26–7, 31,
33, 37, 38, 42, 88–9, 127–8
autobiography of, *see Straight Up*
birth of 13, 16
Bond aspirations of 204
cameos of 135
career turning points of 77–81,
134, 141, 143–4, 146, 148–9
casting agents' views of 120
chat-show appearances of 57, 79,
80, 122–3, 138, 157, 166, 185,
190–2, 194, 195, 198, 202
comedy-panel-show appearances
of 143–4, 165
'Dani' tattoo of 97
depression suffered by 83–4
Dictionary Corner appearance of
144
drama groups attended by 19–21,
22, 24–6, 31
and drug-taking 17, 18–19, 30–1,
40–1, 43, 46, 56, 64, 68–70, 71,
75, 79, 80–1, 82, 83, 84, 86, 91,
100–1, 106–7, 122, 186, 207
#Dyermas hashtag of 172
early film-watching of 17
early life of 13–18
EastEnders' first approach 129,
130, 144
EastEnders joined by 8, 10–11,
149, 164–6, 167, 195, 201
EastEnders' second approach 149
education of 19, 21
fans of 32, 68, 92, 109, 130–1, 136,
146, 197–8, 199
film career of 7, 8–9; *see also*

individual films
and gang culture 14, 21
gay fanbase of 54, 55, 58, 59, 167,
169, 176, 178, 179, 180, 182–6,
202, 208
gay photo shoot of 184–5
girlfriends of 21–2, 31, 36–7, 70–1,
75
and grandfather's death 30, 79, 82
grandmother visits in Spain 104
grandparents looked after by 30
half-siblings of 16, 17
happy-go-lucky nature of 17
hard-man persona of 8, 10, 55, 91,
124, 146, 165, 177–8, 179
homophobia tackled head on by
183–4
and homosexuality 52–3, 54, 55
100-movie goal of 202
ill health of 18
ill-judged comments by 74–5
in Ibiza 68–70
interviews with 41–5, 93, 114,
179–80
'Jack the Lad' life of 70–1
Kelly advises 33
Kermode's attacks on 140
labouring jobs of 37, 46, 96
lead roles of 56
leading-man status of 84, 99, 119,
121, 133
Loose Women appearance of 122
Love delivers wake-up call to 88–9
love of football of 17, 61, 88, 98,
111, 199
Love's on–off relationship with 63,
65–6, 67–8, 87, 106, 110, 113,
115, 124, 126
'low-budget' byword attributed to
139
and marriage 208
as Mick Carter 8, 10
Mirren supports 29

movie-star charisma of 10
and petty crime 18–19, 31
Pinter's influence on 57, 61, 76,
    78–9, 81, 82, 83, 84, 126
poster-boy image of 9
PR manager hired by 129
reality-TV career of 109, 110, 112,
    113, 124–5
repeated faux pas of 108, 122,
    128–9, 130, 137–9, 144
shy nature of 10
singing abilities of 128
Sothcott praises 148
stage fright suffered by 79–80, 81
Strike praises 180
supporting roles of 56, 57
tabloids' treatment of 10, 50, 70,
    78, 83, 91–2, 93, 108, 120, 123,
    127, 128–9, 130, 138, 139, 140,
    142, 155–6, 161, 184, 191
theatre career of, *Certain Young
    Men* 57–9
thirst of, for acting knowledge
    32–3
Treadwell-Collins casts 155–7
trends on Twitter 137
TV debut of 8, 27–30
24th birthday of 79
unemployed status of 57
writing career of 136–9
Dyer Day 172
Dyer, Joanne (partner), *see* Mas,
    Joanne (partner)
Dyer, Kayleigh (sister) 28
    birth of 16
Dyer, Sunnie (daughter) 124, 166
    birth of 121
Dyer, Tony (brother) 16, 28
Dyermas 172

Eames, Dominic 65
EastEnders 15, 46, 65
    Carter family introduced in 155,

158, 162–3, 166, 170–1, 173–
    4, 175, 176, 189, 192–3
Christmas Day 1986 episode of
    152–3
coming-out storyline in 176–88,
    189, 194
creators of 155
DD joins 8, 10–11, 149, 164–6,
    167, 195, 201
DD praises 157
DD's first approach by 129, 130,
    144, 156
DD's second approach by 149
decline of 151–2
fans of 188
first episode of 152
popular characters in 153, 154–5,
    159, 160, 162, 170–1, 186–7,
    196, 198
tagline of 171, 180
three-dimensional overhaul of
    149–50
Treadwell-Collins reinvigorates
    154–5, 157–9, 189, 193, 197,
    199, 207
trends on Twitter 180–1
25th anniversary of 154
30th anniversary of 193
viewing figures 160
EastEnders Ultra 156, 181
eBay 136
Edinburgh International Festival 33
8 Out of 10 Cats 143, 165
Elementary 205
Elizabeth II 14
Elstree Studios 152, 153, 164, 166
Emmerdale 195
Emmy Awards 30
Empire 9, 111, 140
Empire Online 18
Euro 2004 97
Evans, Chris 22, 191
Expendables, The 126

Facebook 183
Faculty, The 53
Family Affairs 153
Fassbender, Michael 9, 113
Fatboy Slim 40
Fawcett Society 137
Female First 118, 127, 142, 143
50 Cent 135
Fila 108
Films of Danny Dyer, The (Sothcott & Mullinger) 39, 41, 44, 45, 46, 52–3, 73, 74, 87, 105, 109, 112, 114, 140, 147, 204
Firm, The 112–13
First World War 47, 48, 49, 50, 55
Fleming, Ian 141
Flynn, Miss 20, 22–3, 24, 191
Flynn, Paul 181, 187
Football Factory, The 87–92, 93, 94, 95, 97, 99, 100, 133
  legacy of 92
  as a love story 90–1
football hooliganism 17, 89–90, 92, 100, 109, 113, 125
Four Weddings and a Funeral 72
Fox TV 205
Fraser, Lady Antonia 79
Freerunner 142–3
French, Michael 154
Friday the 13th 108
Fright Night 17
Front 104
Full Monty, The 71, 72

Gallagher, Noel 71
Game of Thrones 205
Gilbert, Gerard 145
Gill, Peter 57, 58, 59, 184
Girls Aloud 145
Goddard, Ceri 137
Godfather, The 102
Goldman, William 9
Gone in 60 Seconds 74

Goodbye Charlie Bright 65–8, 87, 102
  as a love story 90–1
Goodfellas 101, 104
GQ 172
Grace, Maggie 135
Graham, Jamie 149
Grand National 13
Grand Theft Auto: Vice City 85
Grantham, Leslie 152
Great Ecstasy of Robert Carmichael, The 97
Greenfingers 71–2
Greenwich Borough FC 89
Greenwood, Celia 24–5
Groucho Club 87
Guardian 39, 42–3, 45, 84, 112, 126, 137, 138, 139, 181, 187, 207
  'World of Lather' 172
Guns of Navarone, The 141

Hackney Empire 198
Hampstead Town Hall 24
Happy Valley 205
Harding, Sarah 145
Hardy, Tom 88–9, 113, 133
Harris, Sean 110
Harsh, Jodie 123
Hassan, Tamer 89, 102, 108–9, 110, 111, 134, 135, 142, 205
Hatchard, Danny-Boy 162, 193, 204
Hatosy, Shawn 53–4, 55
Havers, Nigel 159
HBO 205
Hennigan, Adrian 103
Henry, Linda 196–7, 198
Heritage, Stuart 139
Hesmondhalgh, Julie 199
High Heels and Low Lifes 72
Hill, Maddy 162, 170, 175, 191, 199
Holland, Tony 155
Hollyoaks 70
Hollywood 53, 74, 103, 104, 118, 119, 126

Homecoming, The 84, 122
Homeland 205
homophobia 15, 182
Hoskins, Bob 110, 111
Hostel 108
House 205
How Do You Solve a Problem Like Maria? 128
Huffington Post 161, 168
Human Traffic 38, 39–46, 57, 70, 106, 186
    cult status of 68–9
Hunger TV 18, 19, 20, 118, 120, 124, 203, 206

I Believe in UFOs 124–5
Ibiza:
    DD's time in 68
    24/7-party nature of 69
ICF 17
ICM 56
In the Name of the Father 52
In and Out 53
Inbetweeners, The 144
Inception 133
Independent 18, 62, 110, 137–8, 145, 165, 166
Interchange Studios 22, 24–6, 31, 203
    see also WAC Arts
IRA 14, 52
Is Harry On the Boat? 68, 71
ITV 27, 57, 122, 144, 149, 153

Jack Said 136
Jack Says 136
Jackman, Hugh 74
Jacobi, Derek 32
Jaws: The Revenge 125
Jodelka, Filipa 172
Jolie, Angelina 74, 118
Jonah Hex 9
Jonathan Ross Show, The 190
Jones, Ellen E. 163, 165

Jones, Griff Rhys 72
Jones, Vinnie 22, 73, 74, 99
Just for the Record 139

Kay, Peter 159
Keitel, Harvey 33
Kelly, Charlotte 26, 27, 32, 56
Kelly, Craig 33
Kemp, Gary 202–3
Kemp, Martin 202–3
Kermode, Mark 140
Kerrigan, Justin 38, 41–2, 43, 45
Kray, Reggie 15
Kray, Ronnie 15
Krays, The 202
Kurt and Sid 84

lads' mags 105, 109, 113, 136–7, 138
Lady Di (dog) 162, 197
Lady, The 29, 130, 136, 204, 208
Lakes, The 44
Lamb, Larry 153
Last Seven, The 139
Laurie, Hugh 205
Laverne, Lauren 164
Law, Jude 70
Layer Cake (book) 74
Layer Cake (film) 75
Leone, Sergio 104
Les Misérables 25
Lewis, Damian 205
Leyland 14
Lily Allen and Friends 122–3
Lincoln, Andrew 205
Lincoln Center 77
Line of Duty 205
Little, Daran 177, 181
Live Another Day 205
Liverpool FC 13
Lloyd, Gwen 9
Lloyd-Webber, Andrew 128, 129
Loaded 113
Lock, Stock and Two Smoking Barrels

74, 126
London Palladium 128
Long Good Friday, The 111
Longest Yard, The 73
Loose Women 122, 127
Lorraine 127
Love, Nick 63, 77, 88, 89, 90, 97, 98,
     99, 100, 103, 107, 111, 112, 120,
     135, 148, 178, 184
   and alcohol 67
   DD's on–off relationship with 63,
        65–6, 67–8, 87, 106, 110, 113,
        115, 124, 126
   directorial debut of 65–6
   early promise of 105–6
   interviews with 104, 105, 113
   perfectionist nature of 101–2
   stalled career of 87
Love Story 65
Lovefilm.com 7, 10, 119, 148
Loving 34, 35
Lucy, Gary 177

McAvoy, James 118
Macdonald, Kelly 205
Mackintosh, Cameron 128
McKellen, Ian 159
Mail Online 184
Malice in Wonderland 134–5
Manookian, Roland 66, 102, 110
Mas, Joanne (partner) 21–2, 31, 44–
     5, 64, 75, 78, 81, 83, 85, 92, 104,
     106, 107, 116, 118, 119, 121, 122,
     123, 128, 147, 157, 166, 207
   All Star Mr & Mrs appearance of
        122
   DD cheats on 70, 71
   DD gets back with 93, 96
Maysh, Jeff 104
Mean Machine 73–4, 99
Meatpacking District 79
Midsomer Murders 153
Miller, Jonny Lee 28, 70, 205

Millwall FC 89
Mirren, Helen 8, 27, 29, 72
Mirror 78, 93
Misery 9
Mis-Teeq 68
Mr Bean 72
Morris, Mark 42
Morrissey, Neil 145
Moss, Kate 70
Moyer, Stephen 205
MTV 96
Mullinger, James 39, 42, 44, 46, 48,
     74, 109, 112, 140, 141
Murphy, Alan 69
Murphy, Cillian 48

Nagra, Parminder 86
National Front 14
National Lottery 136
National Television Awards (NTAs)
     171
National Theatre 81, 82, 83, 85, 167
Neeson, Liam 9
Neilson, David 199
*Never Mind the Bollocks, Here's the
     Sex Pistols* 14
Never Mind the Buzzcocks 143
Newman, Lorraine 151
Newsbeat 145
Nicholls, Paul 46–7, 48–9, 50, 56–7,
     60, 64–5, 66
   Charlie Milwall (*Borstal Boy*) 54
Nine 9
NME 105
No Man's Land 81–2, 85
Non-Stop 9
Norwich City FC 199
Not Gods But Giants 33, 57
Not the Nine O'Clock News 72
Nuts 105
Nyong'o, Lupita 9

Oasis 68, 71

Observer 105
Office, The 108
O'Grady, Paul 157, 192, 194, 195, 198, 202
OK! 204
Oliver! 128–9
One Show, The 22, 191, 206
Only Fools and Horses 15, 162
Oscars 9, 94
Other Half, The 98
Outlaw 109–12, 113, 141, 174
Owen, Wilfred 48
Oxford English Dictionary (*OED*) 59

Pacino, Al 101
Pinter, Harold 57, 59, 60, 62, 76, 77, 78, 80, 81, 83, 84, 85, 121–2, 126
    cancer diagnosed for 82
    death of 61, 84
Piper, Billie 83
Plan B 113
Plebs 144
Postman, The 53
Prime Suspect 8, 29, 32, 35, 57, 72
    awards won by 30
    DD auditions for 26–7, 30
    first airs 27–8
Princess Bride, The 9
Pulp Fiction 134

Quinn, Anthony 145

racism 14, 15, 110
RADA 59
Radio 1 157
Radio Times 151, 152, 154, 155, 158, 161, 163, 170, 175, 194, 201, 206
Rankin, Ian 205
Real Football Factories, The 109, 112, 113
Red Rum 13
Reed, Dan 115, 116, 117
Reid, Mike 159, 160

Revolver 134, 142
Reynolds, Burt 73, 74
Reynolds, Stephen 147
Richard, Cliff 145
Rickman, Alan 33
Ritchie, Guy 74, 126
Rock and Chips 162
Rolling Stone 108
Room, The 62
Rooney, David 51
Ross, Jonathan 57, 79, 80, 156, 157, 166, 185, 190
Roth, Eli 108
Royal Academy of Dramatic Arts (RADA) 59
Run for Your Wife (film) 144–6
Run for Your Wife (play) 144
Rylance, Mark 35

Salem's Lot 17
Sam (dog) 34
Saving Private Ryan 51
Scarface 105
Scorsese, Martin 101
Screen International 141
Scum 17
Second Generation 86
Second World War 14, 33
Sellebrity Soccer 199
Severance 106–8, 118, 132
Sex Pistols 14
sexuality 52–3
Sheridan, Jim 52
Sheridan, Peter 52
Sick Chirpse 13, 119 Silver Jubilee 14
Simm, John 44
6 Music 164
Sky 68, 133
Smith, Christopher 106, 108
Smith, Mel 72, 73
Snatch 74
Soldier Soldier 31

Solomons, Jason 104
Somme, Battle of the 48
Sothcott, Jonathan 39, 42, 44, 46, 48,
    74, 109, 112, 140, 141, 147, 204
Sound of Music, The 128
Southland 54
Spaghetti Westerns 104–5
Spandau Ballet 202, 203
Spielberg, Steven 125
Star Lane 21
Star Wars 13
Statham, Jason 126
Straight Up (Dyer) 15–18 *passim*,
    19, 21, 23, 27, 30, 33, 37–8, 44,
    49–52 *passim*, 54, 58, 60, 61, 78,
    82, 84, 86, 89, 91, 98, 140–1
    Davinia excised from 83
Straightheads 7, 114, 115–16, 118, 121
Strike, Sam 162, 170, 175, 176, 180,
    185–6, 187, 191, 194
Sun 70, 123, 130, 138, 171, 201
Sundance Film Festival 95
Sunday Mirror 83
Sunday People 84
Supernova Heights 71
Sweat the Small Stuff 165
Sweeney, The (film) 104, 113, 120
Sweeney, The (TV series) 113
Swordfish 74

T.Rex 13
Tabloid 97
Take, The (Cole) 133
Taxi Driver 44
Taylor, Davinia 69–70, 71, 77, 78, 79,
    83–4, 85, 96
    miscarriage suffered by 84
Thatcher, Margaret 14
Thewlis, David 28, 35
This Morning 127
Tinker, Tailor, Soldier, Spy 133
Tookey, Christopher 142
Toronto Film Festival 95

Total Film 118, 125, 127, 146, 149,
    202
Touch of Frost, A 31, 33
Trainspotting (film) 28, 41, 42, 46, 68
Trainspotting (novel) (Welsh) 41
Travers, Peter 108
Travolta, John 74
Treadwell-Collins, Dominic 149, 150,
    151–2, 153, 157, 163, 165–6, 176,
    181, 193, 197, 207
    Carter family created by 155
    DD praises 157, 175
    EastEnders as crowning glory of
        153–4
Trench, The 46, 47, 51, 56
True Blood 205
Turner, Lacey 154
24 205
28 Days Later 139
Twitter 137, 164, 172, 173, 180–1,
    183–4, 194, 197, 199, 204

UK Film Council 94

van Outen, Denise 145
Variety 51
Vaughn, Matthew 74, 75
Vendetta 146–7, 148, 174, 204
Vicious, Sid 84

WAC Arts 24
    see also Interchange Studios
Walking Dead, The 205
Wanted 118
Wardle, Irvine 59
Wasp 94–5
We Still Kill the Old Way 204
Weekly Wipe 173
Welsh, Irvine 41
West Ham FC 17, 61
West, Timothy 162, 187, 192
Where Eagles Dare 141
Whishaw, Ben 48

Whitfield, June 145
Williams, Lia 61
Windsor, Barbara 159
Winstone, Ray 113, 120
Womack, Samantha 154
Woodside Comprehensive 19
Woodyatt, Adam 194
World Cup 2006 111

X-Files, The 7, 116

Yahoo! Lifestyle 144
Young Americans, The 33
YouTube 112

Zoo 109
    DD writes for 136–8, 139
    launch of 136